THE RED BOOK: REFLECTIONS ON C. G. JUNG'S *LIBER NOVUS*

In 2009, W. W. Norton published 'The Red Book', a book written by Jung in 1913–14 but not previously published. Snippets of information about the likely contents of 'The Red Book' had been in circulation for years, and there was much debate and eager anticipation of its publication within the Jungian field and the larger reading public. In 2010, a conference was held at the C. G. Jung Institute of San Francisco which brought together an international group of distinguished scholars in analytical psychology to explore and address critical contextual aspects of 'The Red Book' and to debate its importance for current and future Jungian theory and practice. *The Red Book: Reflections on C. G. Jung's* Liber Novus is based on that conference. The individual papers have been thoroughly revised and updated for this book and address some of the important questions and issues that were raised at that conference in response to the presentation of these papers.

As yet there has been very little published about 'The Red Book'. *The Red Book: Reflections on C. G. Jung's* Liber Novus will contribute to setting the agenda for further research, both scholarly and clinical, in response to Jung's account of his experiences between 1913 and 1914, when arguably, the future course of his entire project was set in motion. This book will be essential reading for any reader interested in the importance of 'The Red Book', analytical psychologists, trainee analysts, those with an interest in the history of ideas and historians.

Thomas Kirsch was President of the International Association of Analytical Psychology from 1989 to 1995, and President of the C. G. Jung Institute of San Francisco from 1976 to 1978. He was a lecturer in the Department of Psychiatry at Stanford University Medical School. He currently works in private practice in California.

George Hogenson is a Jungian analyst in private practice in Chicago. He was President of the C. G. Jung Institute of Chicago from 2007 to 2009 and is on the Executive Committee of the International Association for Analytical Psychology.

THE RED BOOK: REFLECTIONS ON C. G. JUNG'S *LIBER NOVUS*

Edited by Thomas Kirsch and George Hogenson

Routledge
Taylor & Francis Group
LONDON AND NEW YORK

First published 2014
by Routledge
27 Church Road, Hove, East Sussex BN3 2FA

Simultaneously published in the USA and Canada
by Routledge
711 Third Avenue, New York NY 10017

Routledge is an imprint of the Taylor & Francis Group, an informa business

British Library Cataloguing in Publication Data
A catalogue record for this book is available from the British Library

Library of Congress Cataloging in Publication Data
A catalog record for this book has been requested

ISBN: 978–0–415–65995–6 (hbk)
ISBN: 978–0–415–65996–3 (pbk)

Typeset in Garamond
by Keystroke, Station Road, Codsall, Wolverhampton

MIX
Paper from responsible sources
FSC® C013604

Printed and bound by CPI Group (UK) Ltd, Croydon, CR0 4YY

CONTENTS

LIST OF ILLUSTRATIONS

FIGURES

PLATES
(between pages 66 and 67)

NOTES ON CONTRIBUTORS

John Beebe, MD, analyst member and past president of the C. G. Jung Institute of San Francisco, is the founding editor of *The San Francisco Jung Institute Library Journal* (now *Jung Journal: Culture & Psyche*) and the first American co-editor of *The Journal of Analytical Psychology.* He is the author of *Integrity in Depth*, co-author (with Virginia Apperson) of *The Presence of the Feminine in Film*, co-author (with C. Peter Rosenbaum) of *Psychiatric Treatment: Crisis Clinic and Consultation*, and editor of C. G. Jung's *Aspects of the Masculine; Terror, Violence and the Impulse to Destroy;* and *Money, Food, Drink, Fashion and Analytic Training.*

Paul Bishop, DPhil, is Professor of German at the University of Glasgow, Scotland. His publications include *Jung's 'Answer to Job': A Commentary*, *Analytical Psychology and German Classical Aesthetics*, and various papers on aspects of analytical psychology. He is a specialist adviser to *The Journal of Analytical Psychology*, a member of the advisory board of *Spring: A Journal of Archetype and Culture*, and a member of the editorial board of the *International Journal of Jungian Studies.* He was the 2010 speaker in the Zürich Lecture Series on Analytical Psychology.

Joseph Cambray, PhD, is President of the International Association for Analytical Psychology; a faculty member in the Center for Psychoanalytic Studies, Harvard Medical School; an analyst member of the New England Society of Jungian Analysts and the Jungian Psychoanalytic Association of New York. He also serves as consulting editor for *The Journal of Analytical Psychology* and is the author of *Synchronicity: Nature & Psyche in an Interconnected Universe* and co-editor with Linda Carter of *Analytical Psychology: Contemporary Perspectives in Jungian Analysis.*

Ulrich Hoerni is Chief Executive Officer of the Foundation of the Works of C. G. Jung (*Stiftung der Werke von C. G. Jung*, established in 2007). From 2007 through 2009, he was also chairman of the foundation board. Having earned a degree in architecture at the ETH Zürich in 1967, he went on to work until 1994 as an architect in Switzerland and Denmark. From 1981 through 2007, he was a member of the Executive Committee of the Society of Heirs of C. G. Jung (*Erbengemeinschaft C. G. Jung*), serving as its CEO beginning in 1997 and as its chairman beginning in 2004. Since 1994, he has been the delegated manager of archival and editorial questions and in this function has been involved in the planning and preparation of new publications, including among others *The Jung-White Letters, The ETH Lectures, The Red Book*, and the *Jung-Kirsch Letters*.

George Hogenson, PhD, is an analyst member of the Chicago Society of Jungian Analysts, past president of the C. G. Jung Institute of Chicago, a member of the editorial board of the *Journal of Analytical Psychology* and the Executive Committee of the International Association for Analytical Psychology. He holds a PhD in philosophy from Yale University and has also studied at St. Olaf College, the University of Chicago, and Kyoto University (Japan). He is the author of *Jung's Struggle with Freud* and has published numerous papers and book chapters on Jung and analytical psychology.

Thomas Kirsch, MD, is an analyst member and past president of the C. G. Jung Institute of San Francisco and past president of the International Association for Analytical Psychology. He is the author of *The Jungians* and co-editor of a Jungian section in two Psychoanalytic dictionaries as well as the book *Initiation: The Reality of an Archetype*. He is in private practice in Palo Alto, California.

Christine Maillard, Docteur ès Lettres, is professor for German culture and Literature at Université de Strasbourg, France, where she is also head of the interdisciplinary research institution Maison Interuniversitaire des Sciences de l'Homme-Alsace. Her doctoral dissertation on C. G. Jung's *Septem Sermones ad Mortuos* (*Les Sept Sermons aux Morts de Carl Gustav Jung*) was published in 1993 at Presses Universitaires de Nancy. She also contributed about twenty publications on C. G. Jung's work in various journals. Her other major research topics concern the relationship between European and Asiatic culture (*L'Inde vue d'Europe. Histoire d'une rencontre 1750–1950*, Paris 2008). She is an honorary member of the IAAP.

Bou-Yong Rhi, MD, is an analyst member of the Korean Association of Jungian Analysts (KAJA) and director of C. G. Jung Institute of Korea. He is Professor Emeritus, Seoul National University Hospital, where he has served as a professor of psychiatry and psychotherapy for 28 years. He is a diplomate of the C. G. Jung Institute in Zürich, and lectured there and at the Union Theological Seminary in New York on the psychology of shamanism. In 1978, he founded the Korean Study Group for Analytical Psychology. His publications include three volumes of *Studies of Analytical Psychology, Suffering and Healing in Korean Shamanism*, along with numerous articles in the Jungian field on Korean folklore and traditional Eastern thought.

Susan Thackrey, PhD, is an analyst member of the C. G. Jung Institute of San Francisco, with special interests in the mytho-poetic, creativity, and art and literature. She holds degrees in history, philosophy, and English literature as well as in psychology. She was a founding partner in Thackrey and Robertson Gallery, where she was active for many years. Among other projects, she wrote the catalogue for the first West Coast exhibition of William Blake's illustrations for the Book of Job. A widely published poet, her books are *Empty Gate* and *George Oppen: A Radical Practice*. Recently she was a keynote speaker and reader at SUNY Buffalo's Centennial Conference on Oppen and opening plenary speaker at the Art and Psyche Conference.

INTRODUCTION TO FIRST REFLECTIONS: INITIAL RESPONSES TO C. G. JUNG'S *RED BOOK (LIBER NOVUS)*

Based on essays presented in San Francisco, 4–6 June 2010

Thomas Kirsch

The Red Book, Jung's personal diary of his confrontation with the unconscious, has now been published, ninety-five years after it was written. Beginning in the autumn of 1913 and essentially finishing by April 1914, he wrote his visions, fantasies, and dreams in a series of black books. Later, he transferred his writings to a large leather-bound Red Book and added medieval-style calligraphy and a series of mandala paintings. Those in the Jungian community have been aware of the existence of this Red Book, but very few outside the family had actually seen it. Now, after over a decade of editorial work by Sonu Shamdasani, and with the cooperation of the Jung estate, we have this beautifully illustrated magnificent *Red Book*. Jung himself was unsure whether to publish it out of concern for his scientific reputation. In today's world, however, it has been fabulously received.

The Red Book gives us a picture of the raw material from which Jung developed most of his mature writings. Reading it is not an easy task. I myself could only stay with the material for a short period of time before I needed a break. I have heard from many others whose experience of reading *The Red Book* has been similar. It came out on 7 October 2009, and many of us are dipping into it a little bit at a time. I find it to be like my first encounter with Jung's writings on alchemy, which made little sense to me initially. Over these many years I have come to appreciate and understand why he used alchemical language to describe the modern unconscious process. I am hoping that over time I will have the same experience with *The Red Book*.

There is no question that *The Red Book* is an important first step toward Jung's own individuation and rediscovery of his soul. Let me give you the context in which Jung began to have spontaneous visions in the autumn of 1913. In January of that year he and Freud had broken off their personal relationship. They had seen one another in September 1913 in Munich at the International Psychoanalytic Congress, but they did not speak to each other. Jung was president of the International Psychoanalytic Association, editor of the *Jahrbuch*, and still considered himself a psychoanalyst. It was a time of transition in many senses, both personally and intellectually for Jung and collectively for the world. He mourned the loss of his relationship to Freud, and, as he recounts in *Memories, Dreams, Reflections*, 'Toward the autumn of 1913 the pressure which I had felt was in *me* seemed to be moving outward, as if there were something in the air' (1963: 175). The winds of World War I were in the air. The visions began on a short train ride to visit his wife's family, and although they occurred over a relatively short period of time, he was to work over these fantasies through inner dialogue, painting, and medieval calligraphy until 1928 when he lay aside the project. What enabled him to stop working on *The Red Book* was a synchronous event. He had painted a mandala with a castle in the center, and it felt to him as though it were distinctively Chinese. He writes in *MDR*, 'In 1928, when I was painting this picture, showing the golden, well-fortified castle, Richard Wilhelm in Frankfurt sent me the thousand-year old Chinese text on the yellow castle, the germ of the immortal body.' It was *The Secret of the Golden Flower*, a Chinese alchemical Taoist work, in which he found images and texts quite like the ones that he had been working with in his own Red Book. This relieved him of his isolation. In the 1950s, he attempted to return to the Red Book, but he stopped in midsentence and never picked it up again.

The essays in this book are initial attempts at an interpretation from important scholars in the field of analytical psychology, although I suspect that a definitive interpretation of *The Red Book* may never be possible. They were presented at a conference in San Francisco, California, on 4–6 June 2010. The conference was sponsored by the Extended Education Committee of the C. G. Jung Institute of San Francisco to celebrate the publication of *The Red Book*. Each author is deeply involved in Jung studies, and together they present a wide variety of viewpoints.

Ulrich Hoerni, one of Jung's grandsons and the member of the Jung family most responsible for the publication of *The Red Book*, started us out on the first full day of talks. Hoerni is the head of the Jung family's foundation, which was set up to oversee publication of Jung's unpublished works, and he has studied Jung's works deeply. Here, he relates the history and development of *The Red Book* project.

The keynote speaker was Paul Bishop, professor of German at the University of Glasgow and a well-known Jungian scholar and author. His essay discusses the relationship of Goethe, Schiller, and German Romanticism to reading *The Red Book*, revealing how Jung's language is amazingly similar to Goethe's in his epic *Faust.*

He was followed by Joseph Cambray, president of the IAAP and a much-published author in the Jungian world. His essay is a fascinating amplification of Jung's paintings from a dream of the radiolarian, a form of jelly fish, in relationship to the biological illustrations of Ernst Haeckel from the turn of the twentieth century. There is an amazing similarity between the Haeckel images of the radiolarian and Jung's mandala paintings from his dream.

The third lecture of the morning was delivered by Bou-Young Rhi, professor of psychiatry at Seoul National University, a Jungian analyst, and founder of the Jung Study Group in Korea. His essay discusses Korean shamanism and its relationship to the mandala symbolism in Jung.

In the afternoon, our first lecturer was Susan Thackrey, a former art gallery owner, historian, poet, and now a Jungian analyst in San Francisco. Her essay discusses and interprets much of the art that Jung painted for his Red Book. There are fifty-three full-page mandalas reproduced in the published *Red Book*.

The next speaker of the afternoon was Christine Maillard, professor of medieval philosophy in Strasbourg, France, and the translator of *The Red Book* into French. She is a leading expert on Jung and Gnosticism, and in her essay, she speaks about Jung's *Seven Sermons to the Dead*, which had previously been published separately as an appendix to *Memories, Dreams, Reflections*.

The following morning the conference concluded with two presentations. George Hogenson, co-editor of these essays, presented imagery and literature from Western medieval philosophy, relating it to modern science. Hogenson has a PhD in philosophy and is a Jungian analyst in Chicago. His essay is complex, brilliantly written, and introduces the reader to many unfamiliar and esoteric names in Western philosophy.

The final speaker of the conference was John Beebe, a well-known Jungian analyst from San Francisco, who in his essay invokes the trickster archetype, comparing Jung's inner journey in *The Red Book* to Cervantes' famous figure of Don Quixote.

The conference was a truly memorable event with an overflow audience. All the participants have been waiting for over two years to read these papers. We hope this volume will reach an equally enthusiastic reading audience.

Reference

Jung, C. G. (1963) *Memories, Dreams, Reflections*, recorded and edited by Aniela Jaffe, New York: Random House.

1

THE GENESIS OF *THE RED BOOK* AND ITS PUBLICATION

Ulrich Hoerni

I first presented this paper at the invitation of The C. G. Jung Institute of San Francisco in June 2010, when they kindly invited me to talk about the genesis of *The Red Book* and its publication. I was informed that attendees were 'looking to this conference as a "way in" to *The Red Book* – a way of making it less intimidating and more accessible . . . – yet also that only a small number . . . would have actually read the entire book.' Whereas many would 'have read some parts of it, some might have basically only looked at the images, and a few [would] not have read anything but are curious.' Perhaps the same holds true for readers of this book.

As I took part in the preparation of the edition on behalf of C. G. Jung's heirs, I would like to present a summary of the developments and considerations that led to the publication of *The Red Book.* In retrospect, this is easy. We faced a great many unanswered questions when we started working. And I can't claim that we have a complete overview of the book's various aspects today. *The Red Book* is a unique work in many respects. Still, it did not simply fall out of the sky but emerged from a certain historical and intellectual context. It probably can't be understood in and of itself. I will, therefore, also address *contextual* questions regarding its genesis, its effect, and its editing.

To begin, we must look to the year 1913, which was pivotal for Jung. The preliminary events are well known: From 1901–9, Jung worked as a psychiatrist at the Burghölzli clinic; from 1906 onward, he successfully introduced psychoanalysis there and worked together with Freud, although not to treat patients, but to build the International Psychoanalytical Association, organize congresses, and edit yearbooks. From 1909 onward, he had his own private practice. He also gave lectures on psychoanalysis at the University of Zürich. It looked as if he was going to have a successful academic career, but it turned out otherwise. Jung realized that he did not share all of Freud's views. They seemed to him reductionist, rationalistic, and backward-looking, oriented to the social morality of the nineteenth century; at the same time, they seemed to lack religious and philosophical dimensions. Similar reservations applied to the materialistic and causal thinking of the orthodox sciences. Jung's book *Transformations and Symbols of the Libido* led to a conflict between the two men. In January 1913, Freud ended the private relationship. In October 1913, Jung quit his collaboration on the yearbook. In April 1914, he resigned from his post as president of the International Psychoanalytical Association and as a lecturer at the university. It is not inappropriate to talk of a setback in his career or even a midlife crisis.

For Jung, there now began – I quote – 'a period of inner uncertainty [. . .] It would be no exaggeration to call it a state of disorientation' (Jung 1963: 170). He was increasingly haunted by impressive dreams and strong emotions. To find his bearings, he commenced the by now famous experiment that lasted until about 1930 and became known as his 'Confrontation with the Unconscious.' It was the development of a technique to 'get to the bottom of [his] inner processes,' 'to translate the emotions into images,' 'to grasp the fantasies which were stirring . . . "underground"' (178). He later called this method *active imagination.* He first recorded these fantasies in his *Black Books.* He then revised these texts at least three times, added reflections on them, and copied them in a calligraphic script, accompanied by his own paintings, into a book bound in red leather. In 1930, Jung ended his experiment and put *The Red Book* aside – unfinished. So much about the book's genesis. Jung started to write *about* the experiment from early on, as is well documented today: The essay 'The Transcendent Function' outlines the technique of active imagination; *Memories, Dreams, Reflections* describes how he personally perceived it, and with *The Red Book*, we can now also see the results of his work.

But what is the actual content of *The Red Book*? It would be presumptuous if I tried, in this paper, to present you with any form of quintessence. Going through and understanding *The Red Book* must be your own task. I would, however, at least like to point out certain structures and patterns to facilitate access. The text starts with a surprising title, 'The Way of What Is to Come,' accompanied by a compilation of quotations from the Bible, beginning with Isaiah:

> Isaiah said: The wilderness and the solitary place shall be glad for them; and the desert shall rejoice, and blossom as the rose. It shall blossom abundantly, and rejoice even with joy and singing. . . . Then the eyes of the blind shall be opened, and the ears of the deaf shall be unstopped. Then shall the lame man leap as a hart, and the tongue of the dumb sing: for in the wilderness shall waters break out, and streams in the desert. And the parched ground shall be a pool, and the thirsty land springs of water: in the habitation of dragons, where each lay, shall be grass with reeds and rushes. And a highway shall be there, and a way, and it shall be called The way of holiness; [. . .]
>
> (Isaiah 35:1–8)[1]

After so much rejoicing, we are, obviously, not presented with a case history or chaotic and embarrassing therapeutic material, as has been suspected, but with the outlines of a *way,* an *intention,* a *program,* even a *vision.* First, Jung explains how the experiment came about. Although he has reached 'honour, power, wealth, knowledge, and every human happiness,' he suffers from the loss of his soul (2009: 231). The first chapter is, therefore, entitled 'Refinding the Soul,' and once Jung has happily found her again, he starts a kind of journey with her. This is the overall motif of the work. Jung strolls through picturesque landscapes meeting strange characters, among them Satan himself, and has profound conversations with them. On these occasions, he is not the one who dispenses wisdom, but the one who asks questions. Chapters always begin with imagined scenes – images, dialogues, sensations, emotions. These scenes are then commented on, along the lines of 'what can we learn from this?' The stringing together of single episodes refers to a literary genre with a long tradition of which the *Odyssey* or *Hans im Glück*[2] are representatives. Jung's text ends with the words, 'This is the way' (330). One could ask whether *The Red Book* reaches a conclusion. Maybe the journey and its single episodes are the reward.

Jung's conversations are, of course, not about everyday business, but literally about God and the world, life and death, heaven and hell; in other words, existential questions from an area in which psychology, philosophy, art, and religion merge, an area that will be the breeding ground of analytical psychology. For people acquainted with this, it may not be without appeal to see, so to speak, Jung's ideas in their embryonic state, such as the typology, the shadow and its acceptance, the self, the understanding of the symbol, the process of individuation, and many other things. The acting characters represent – of course – archetypes. The dialogues and comments are riddled with explicit and implicit allusions to philosophical, mythological, and religious literature. Prime examples are the New Testament and Nietzsche's works. The melodious names of the characters – Elijah, Salomé, Izdubar, Philemon, Ammonius, Telesphoros, and others – do not arise from Jung's imagination but from literature. The text of *The Red Book* is thus a multilayered, comprehensive composition that places great demands on the reader.

The paintings are a different case: they immediately impress with their beauty and charisma. Yet the paintings and text do not form a homogenous entity. There isn't a corresponding text passage for each painting. One also notices that different types of paintings can be distinguished. A first type, richly illuminated initials, are literally intertwined with the text. A second, fairly rare type are paintings that actually illustrate the text. A third type tell, as independent chapters, separate stories in the form of an illustration with a short text. A fourth and frequent type stands alone with no reference to the text. This is particularly the case with a series of mandalas.

What was the experiment's further development? Jung shared his inner experiences with some close associates. In his 1925 seminars on analytical psychology, he described his confrontation with the unconscious. But after 1930 he let the Red Book rest for decades. Meanwhile, the insights he had gained through it directly informed his subsequent writings. With his senses sharpened by his own development, he now began to study similar psychic processes. His experiences found particular expression in his seminars about inner images. From 1930 to 1934, he held the so-called *German Seminars,* the *Kundalini Yoga Seminar,* and the famous *Visions Seminars,* and from 1938 to 1941, he presented an entire series of lectures on this subject, including active imagination, eastern and western meditation, and alchemy.

Although Jung actively considered publishing *The Red Book,* he never took the necessary steps. In 1916, he privately published the *Seven Sermons to the Dead,* a short work that arose from the same context. Even the 1916 essay, 'The Transcendent Function,' in which he described the technique of active imagination, was only published in 1958. He mentioned the reasons why he did not publish *The Red Book:* it was unfinished; his growing interest in alchemy as a research topic had distracted him from his work on it; and he called the detailed working out of his fantasies in *The Red Book* a necessary but annoying 'aestheticizing elaboration.' As late as 1957, Jung declared that the *Black Books* and *The Red Book* were autobiographical records that he did not want published in his *Collected Works* since they were not of a scholarly character. As a concession, he allowed Aniela Jaffé to quote excerpts in *Memories, Dreams, Reflections.* In 1959, he – surprisingly – tried to complete the text of *The Red Book* with the help of the old draft and to finish an incomplete painting. He also started on an epilogue, but both the calligraphic text and epilogue break off in midsentence.

In 1961, Jung died. For his descendants, the inheritance of Jung's literary rights brought an obligation and challenge: to see through the publication of the German edition of his *Collected Works*. In his will, Jung had expressed the wish that *The Red Book* and the *Black Books* should remain with his family, without, however, giving more detailed instructions. Because *The Red Book* was not meant to be published in the *Collected Works,* the heirs concluded that this was Jung's final wish concerning the work and that it was an entirely private matter. They did not consider further publications. In 1984, the newly appointed executive committee had five photographic duplicates made. For the first time, Jung's descendants now had the opportunity to take a close look at it. When, after 1990, the editing of the German *Collected Works* was drawing to a conclusion, the executive committee decided to start looking through all the accessible unpublished material with an eye to additional publications. It turned out that there was an entire corpus of drafts and variants pertaining to *The Red Book.* Yet whether and how this substantial material could be published remained an open question. At first glance, style and content appeared to have little in common with Jung's other works. Much was unclear, and by the mid-1990s, there was no one left who could provide firsthand information on these points.

However, since Jung's time, the *history* of psychology had been gaining in importance and could now offer a new approach. In connection with the edition of the *Kundalini Yoga Seminar,* I had come in contact with Sonu Shamdasani. In extensive talks, we discussed the possibility of further Jung publications, both in general terms as well as with regard to *The Red Book.* The book had emerged in a specific context with which a reader at the turn of the twenty-first century is no longer familiar. But a historian of psychology would be able to present it as a historical document. With the help of primary sources, he could embed it in the cultural context of its genesis, situate it within the history of science, and relate it to Jung's life and works. In 1999, Sonu Shamdasani compiled these guiding principles. On the basis of his proposal, the Society of Heirs decided in the spring of 2000 – not without discussion – to release *The Red Book* for publication and to hand over the task of editing it to Sonu Shamdasani.

It was an interesting and unusual task. Apart from *The Red Book,* we were not only confronted with archival material pertaining to it, but also with many open questions about which we would have liked to have asked the author himself. Editing *The Red Book*, therefore, meant more than simply preparing a text for publication; it required a great amount of research. To begin with, several hundred manuscript pages had to be transcribed and the transcription needed to be checked again. My daughter and I took part in this job. Sonu Shamdasani compared the different text variants line by line to shed light on Jung's way of composing his text. In the ETH and the family archives, countless letters from that period were scanned for relevant information. Of great importance was the inspection of Jung's library at Küsnacht with regard to works that could have served as sources of information or inspiration. It turned out not only that such works existed, but also that the library, with its holdings on psychology, mythology, religions, cults, ethnology, history, archaeology, and much more, was at least in part a near mirror image of *The Red Book.* From countless pieces, Sonu Shamdasani finally assembled a contextual background mosaic for *The Red Book.* A special challenge was the rendition of Jung's solemn and somewhat archaic language into an English translation. A team of three translators, Mark Kyburz, John Peck, and Sonu Shamdasani, from the Philemon Foundation tackled this exceedingly delicate task.

The desire to have *The Red Book*'s content *interpreted* played an important role. Together with the editor, however, it was decided to refrain from interpretation and to provide *source material* only. The publication should not present the final answer to all riddles, but should supply a good basis for further studies. Also, Jung's own views should come into play as often as possible, which is why the edition contains not only the material of *The Red Book* itself, but also further texts and fragments by Jung and the already mentioned contextual references. The published edition was planned as a kind of work report. We assume that competent interpretations will be given in forthcoming secondary literature.

Behind all our endeavors and decisions were two related questions: What *is The Red Book?* And why would someone want to embark on such an enterprise? There was no secret knowledge in the family, but at least there was a group of people who had known Jung personally. Despite his pondering of highly complex questions concerning the human mind, he also had a considerable amount of common sense. It is hard to imagine that with the huge *Red Book* he wanted to attach such physical importance to his dreams and fantasies themselves, or that he wanted to express, as has been suspected, his grief about the unsatisfactory end of his relationship with Freud or even Sabina Spielrein. In 1956, Jung wrote in a letter to Eugen Böhler:

> Man and his soul, the individual, is the only real carrier of life, who doesn't just work, eat, sleep, reproduce, and die but also has a meaningful destiny reaching far beyond him. And for this we have no 'myth' any more.
>
> This was the question that raised its menacing head in 1912, when I put the full stop to my manuscript of *Transformations and Symbols of the Libido*. The attempt to answer it led me straight into the unconscious, for only the psyche itself can provide the answer.
>
> (1975: 286)

Shortly after this, he made his famous statement, which became the motto for *The Red Book*'s publication:

> The years when I was pursuing my inner images were the most important in my life – in them everything essential was decided. It all began then; the later details are only supplements and clarifications of the material that burst forth from the unconscious, and at first swamped me. It was the prima materia for a lifetime's work.
>
> (2009: vii)

And this lifetime's work was, in Jung's case, analytical psychology. Despite its seemingly subjective character, *The Red Book* is thus not a personal but a *professional* matter. Analytical psychology posits certain new, basic assumptions, such as the collective unconscious. Since about 1970, a particular expression has been in use, which Jung knew but would not yet use in that sense: *paradigm*. *The Red Book* would thus be a poetic vision of a paradigm shift in psychotherapy. A vision, it has to be added, which had its origin almost a hundred years ago. Jung worked on *The Red Book* for 16 years. The editing process took about 10. I hope I have been able to give you a general idea of *The Red Book*'s development in this brief introduction.

Notes

1 Jung used Luther's German Translation of the Bible; English renderings are from the King James Version.

2 *Hans im Glück* (*Hans in Luck*) is a tale collected by the Brothers Grimm, recounting the adventurous travels of a youth named Hans and his eventual return to his home.

References

Jung, C. G. (2009) *The Red Book: Liber Novus*, ed. Sonu Shamdasani, trans. Mark Kyburz, John Peck, and Sonu Shamdasani, New York: W. W. Norton and Co.

Jung, C. G. (1963) *Memories, Dreams, Reflections*, ed. Aniela Jaffé, trans. Richard Winston, and Clara Winston, New York: Random House.

Jung, C. G. (1975) *C. G. Jung Letters, Volume 2: 1951–1961*, ed. Gehard Adler, Aniela Jaffé, Trans. R. F. C. Hull, Princeton: Princeton University Press.

2

JUNG AND THE QUEST FOR BEAUTY

The Red Book in relation to German classicism

Paul Bishop

One has – perhaps inevitably – almost a sense of trepidation when writing about *The Red Book*.[1] Its editor, Sonu Shamdasani, has counseled that people spend at least a year immersing themselves in the work before beginning to write about it (Henderson 2009: 191), and he warned that commentators are likely to find in it no more than a confirmation of their preconceptions (Horton 2009). Yet *The Red Book* is, of all Jung's works, the one that most forcibly compels us to speak – or at least to gasp, to be amazed, to cry out in wonder or incomprehension. It is a book that elicits an immediate, even an involuntary response from anyone who sees it, and yet it is not a book one would like to read in the dark by candlelight on one's own.

So it is important at the outset to emphasize that approaching *The Red Book* through its relation to German classicism is not an attempt to reduce *The Red Book* to a known quantity or to something readily identifiable. Rather, just as *The Red Book* shows us a very different aspect of Jung, unlike the conventional figure to whom we have become accustomed, so we should try to think of German classicism aside from the conventions and expectations, the preformed opinions and even prejudices, that contaminate this label. In a sense, *The Red Book* takes us to the heart of German classicism. For it is a quest for beauty – for 'the beauty in me and with myself' (RB: 323).

In this respect, or so it seems to me, *The Red Book* confirms and strengthens the case for reading Jung within the context of his European and Germanic cultural inheritance – one that includes German classicism. Nevertheless, placing Jung's work in general and his *Red Book* in particular in a Germanic, European cultural context is emphatically *not* intended to lend a false sense of familiarity to Jung's project or to make it more comfortable to engage with. Instead, the defamiliarization, the book's very strangeness, and the palpable sense of alienation that Jung's *Red Book* awakens, can serve as an invitation to look afresh at German and European culture, and at German classicism specifically, and to rediscover their relevance for today's experience of what, in the opening of *Liber Primus*, 'The Way of What is to Come,' Jung calls 'the spirit of the age' and 'the spirit of the depths' (RB: 229).

Indeed, one of these two terms, 'the spirit of the age' or *der Geist dieser Zeit*, may be borrowed, as Shamdasani's editorial apparatus notes (RB: 229, note 5), from Goethe: the expression *der Geist der Zeiten* can be found in one of the earlier scenes from *Faust*, Part One (specifically, ll. 577–9). It is important to realize, however, how Jung's use of this phrase moves beyond the level of the purely allusive or the merely quotational, to engage with the substance of the scene in which it is used. In 'Night,' we see Wagner, Faust's academic assistant, engaged in conversation with his frustrated master, the man-of-learning who realizes he really knows nothing. At one point, Wagner self-contentedly tells Faust:

> Excuse me, but it's very pleasant
> Studying epochs other than the present,
> Entering their spirit, reading what they say,
> And seeing how much wiser we have grown today.
>
> *Verzeiht! es ist ein groß Ergetzen,*
> *Sich in den Geist der Zeiten zu versetzen;*
> *Zu schauen, wie vor uns ein weiser Mann gedacht,*
> *Und wie wir's dann zuletzt so herrlich weit gebracht.*[2]
>
> (*Faust*, Part One, ll. 570–3; Goethe 1987a: 21)

– to which Faust replies:

> Oh yes indeed, a wisdom most sublime! –
> My friend, the spirit of an earlier time,
> To us it is a seven-sealed mystery;
> And what you learned gentleman would call
> Its spirit, is its image, that is all,
> Reflected in your own mind's history.
> And what a sight it often is!
>
> *O ja, bis an die Sterne weit!*
> *Mein Freund, die Zeiten der Vergangenheit*
> *Sind uns ein Buch mit sieben Siegeln.*
> *Was ihr den Geist der Zeiten heißt,*
> *Das ist im Grund der Herren eigner Geist,*
> *In dem die Zeiten sich bespiegeln.*
> *Da ist's denn wahrlich oft ein Jammer!*
>
> (*Faust I*, ll. 574–80; Goethe 1987: 21)

Here, Faust levels at Wagner the same accusation that, earlier in the scene, the Earth Spirit had leveled at him:

> THE SPIRIT. You are like the spirit you comprehend:
> I am not he. [*It vanishes.*]
>
> GEIST. *Du gleichst dem Geist, den du begreifst,*
> *Nicht mir!* Verschwindet.
>
> (*Faust I*, ll. 512–13; Goethe 1987: 19)

and anticipates his lament at the insufficiency of Wagner's intellectual and emotional ambitions:

> How does the mind sustain some hope and pleasure
> That's stuck forever to the same old terms,
> With greedy fingers grubbing after treasure,
> And gratified to dig up worms!
>
> *Wie nur dem Kopf nicht alle Hoffnung schwindet,*
> *Der immerfort an schalem Zeuge klebt,*
> *Mit gier'ger Hand nach Schätzen gräbt,*
> *Und froh ist, wenn er Regenwürmer findet!*
>
> (*Faust I*, ll. 602–5; Goethe 2001: 18)

In other words, *der Geist dieser Zeit* in Jung's *Red Book* is only indirectly related to *der Geist der Zeiten*, as referred to in *Faust*. In *The Red Book*, *der Geist der Zeit[en]* is presented in opposition to something much richer: *der Geist der Tiefe* or 'the spirit of the depths,' a spirit that stands in a relationship of correspondence to political events at the time of Jung's visions (that is to say, the run-up to the outbreak of the First World War) (RB: 230–1).[3]

Nevertheless, Faust articulates the animating principles behind Goethe's entire drama, and behind the whole of Jung's *Red Book* as well, when in the opening scene entitled 'Night' he says:

> To grant me a vision of Nature's sources
> That bind the world, all its seeds and sources
> And innermost life – all this I shall see,
> And stop peddling in words that mean nothing to me.
>
> *Daß ich erkenne, was die Welt*
> *Im Innersten zusammenhält,*
> *Schau' alle Wirkenskraft und Samen,*
> *Und tu' nicht mehr in Worten kramen.*
>
> (*Faust I*, ll. 382–5; Goethe 1987: 15)

Subsequently, in conversation with Wagner, Faust declares in a way that underlines the importance that *The Red Book* teaches about engagement with the soul:

> What you don't feel, you won't hunt down by art,
> Unless it wells from your inward source,
> And with contentment's elemental force
> Takes sway of every hearer's heart.
> [. . .]
> But never heart to heart will you be joining
> Unless you let your own heart speak.
> [. . .]
> From naught can you refreshment wring
> Unless from your own inmost soul it burst.
>
> *Wenn ihr's nicht fühlt, ihr werdet's nicht erjagen,*
> *Wenn es nicht aus der Seele dringt*
> *Und mit urkräftigem Behagen*
> *Die Herzen aller Hörer zwingt.*
> [. . .]
> *Doch werdet ihr nie Herz zu Herzen schaffen,*
> *Wenn es euch nicht von Herzen geht.*
> [. . .]
> *Erquickung hast du nicht gewonnen,*
> *Wenn sie dir nicht aus eigner Seele quillt.*
> (*Faust I*, ll. 534–7; 544–5; 568–9; Goethe 2001: 16–17)

In turn, *The Red Book* tells us in 'Descent into Hell in the Future': 'The spirit of the depths opened my eyes and I caught a glimpse of the inner things, the world of my soul, the many-formed and changing' (RB: 237); and in 'Soul and God,' Jung reflects: 'Scholarliness is not enough; there is a knowledge of the heart that gives deeper insight' (*Denn Gelehrsamkeit allein genügt nicht; es gibt ein Wissen des Herzens, das tiefere Aufschlüsse gibt*) (233).

In other words, it is important to understand that *The Red Book* is related to German classicism in different ways, among which it is important to distinguish. Ultimately, three major themes allow us to classify *The Red Book* as a document of classicism, in the sense that the term is defined by Adrian Stokes: as 'spring[ing] from a precise love and a passionate identification with what is other,' as 'insisting on an order there, strong, enduring and final *as being an other being*,' as 'untainted by the overt gesture, without the summary treatment, without the *arrière pensée* of "thinking makes it so"' (1947: 174; cited in Stephenson 2010: 90). These themes are: first, its insistence on reality – on the reality of the psyche; second, the goal of wholeness; and third, its doctrine of the acceptance of limitation. At the same time, distinguishing among various modes of relationship helps us to appreciate the complex, yet vital, relationship between *The Red Book* and German classicism.

To begin, there is a mode of relation we might describe as the *formal*. When the press release of the Philemon Foundation appeared, it compared *The Red Book* to *The Book of Kells* and the illuminated works of William Blake (Philemon Foundation 2009; Horton 2009), and it is at once both of these – and more: it is Jung's attempt to produce his equivalent of Goethe's *Faust* and Nietzsche's *Zarathustra*, as well as his attempt to produce an equivalent of Homer's *Odyssey*, Virgil's *Aeneid*, the Gospels (canonical *and* apocryphal), Wolfram von Eschenbach's *Parzival*, Dante's *Divina Commedia*, and Wagner's *Ring* – all in one go and in a single volume (which is presented as a medieval illuminated manuscript). At the same time, the fascination with calligraphy reflects Stefan George's concern about writing in a script unique to himself; the obsession with layout and different sizes of lettering is reminiscent of Stéphane Mallarmé's poetic exercise in self-referential typography, *Un Coup de dés*. (As Mallarmé himself said, *tout, au monde, existe pour aboutir à un livre* – 'everything in the world exists to go into a book' – and *The Red Book* is just such a book [1945: 382]). Equally, one might add, as well as echoing the past, *The Red Book* is in many ways a forward-looking document, anticipating Alan Ginsberg's *Howl* and the drug-fueled fantasies of the entire Beat Generation (those 'angelheaded hipsters burning for the ancient heavenly connection'), or the sham antiquities of J. R. R. Tolkien. One could imagine some parts of *The Red Book* had been written to be set to music by Carl Orff . . . Above all, *The Red Book* represents an attempt on Jung's part to engage in text and image – one might say, although this is a problematic term, to which I shall return, to engage *aesthetically* – with the psyche, with the soul, with the self.

Just as Goethe, the poet, novelist, and dramatist, wrote scientific works, which he considered to be the most important part of his output, so conversely Jung, the scientist, the psychologist, the phenomenologist – the maker of a modern psychology, so Shamdasani has elsewhere argued (2003)[4] – turns to painting,[5] to architecture and sculpture (his tower at Bollingen and his sculptures there),[6] to poetry,[7] and to the visual and literary exercise of *The Red Book*, in order to carry out his investigation into the depths of the psyche and into the inner sources of the self.

Second, there is a mode of relation one could describe as *methodological*. For *The Red Book* interrogates the relation between Art and Nature, between Art and Science, between Art and Life, linking to a number of doubts about the validity of Jung's enterprise in *The Red Book* expressed in *Memories, Dreams, Reflections*. In general, we may say that Jung, while operating with the same categories, has a tendency to distinguish and separate out what, for German classicism, belongs together. In the opening line of one of his sonnets, Goethe famously remarks: *Natur und Kunst, sie scheinen sich zu fliehen* ('Nature, it seems, must always clash with Art'), before insisting that, in fact, they belong together: *Und haben such, eh man es denkt, gefunden* ('And yet, before we know it, both are one') (Goethe 1983: 164–5).

These two simple lines shine a powerful light on a number of paragraphs in *Memories, Dreams, Reflections*, the frequent references to which in Shamdasani's commentary on *The Red Book*, in a sense, rehabilitate this text (not as an historical objective source of biographical information, but as a subjective expression of what Jung thought he was doing).[8] In *Memories, Dreams, Reflections*, we find the suggestion that Jung, as he recorded his fantasies – transcribing them in the *Black Books*, and elaborating and painting them in *The Red Book* – remained uncertain as to the nature of his activity. According to this account (which is corroborated by E. A. Bennet in his record of his own conversations with Jung), even as he was painting, drawing, and writing, Jung was asking himself: 'What am I really doing? Certainly this has nothing to do with science. But what then is it?,' at which point Jung heard a female voice saying 'it is art' (Jung 1983: 210).[9] (Subsequent researchers have suggested that the female voice can be identified as that of Sabina Spielrein [Carotenuto 1982; Kerr 1994: 502–7] or of Maria Moltzer [Shamdasani 1992: 129].)

Jung was keen to reject the voice's conclusion and, in a later imaginary dialogue, during which it again maintained, 'that is art,' he angrily retorted, 'no, it is not; on the contrary, it is nature' (MDR: 210).[10] For Jung, it seems, it was vital to reject the idea his experiences were aesthetic ones, yet equally important to insist on their validity in psychological terms, as if these were mutually exclusive categories: but are they really? In *Memories, Dreams, Reflections*, we find a clear condemnation of this classification of his experiences in terms of art, for this would, it is argued, rob them of moral responsibility. Had Jung regarded 'the fantasies of the unconscious' as art, so this argument goes, then he would have been able to contemplate them with his 'inner eye' (*inneren Auge*) or 'as if watching a film'; and in this case, they would have carried no more conviction than any other 'sense perception' (*Sinneswahrnehmung*), and he would have felt no 'ethical obligation' (*ethische Verpflichtung*) toward them (MDR: 212). I shall return to this important notion of the 'ethical obligation' to images later in this discussion.

A third mode of relation is what we might call the *quotational* mode, in which we find explicit allusions and references to German literature – to Goethe, to Schiller, and to Nietzsche – as well as less obvious echoes and paraphrases. Most (but not all) of these are identified by Shamdasani in his editorial apparatus. For example, after his first conversation with the tramp in 'One of the Lowly' in *Liber Secundus*, there is an explicit reference to Schiller's *Wilhelm Tell* (RB: 265). Then again, there are explicit references to Nietzsche and to the death of God (293, 298, 348), as well as numerous rhetorical echoes of *Zarathustra* (229–30, 249, 297, 309, 316).

As for Goethe, Jung doffs his cap (as it were) to *Faust* on a number of occasions; I have already mentioned the motif of the 'spirit of the age,' but there are several others. At the beginning of *Liber Secundus*, when talking about the Red One as the devil, or *his* devil,[11] Jung identifies him with his 'joy,' with 'that strong joy of that world that comes unsuspected like a warm southerly wind with swelling fragrant blossoms and the ease of living' (*der Leichtigkeit des Lebens*),[12] adding in the *Draft:* 'You have heard from Faust how commanding this kind of joy is' (RB: 260, note 13). 'Whoever tastes this joy,' Jung continues, 'forgets himself,' noting again in his *Draft:* 'As you have known from Faust, there are many who forget who they were because they let themselves be swept away' (260, note 14). Similarly, in the final chapter of *Liber Secundus*, entitled 'The Magician,' the names of the magician and his wife, ΦΙΛΗΜΩΝ and ΒΑΥΚΙΣ, derive from Ovid via *Faust* (RB: 312).[13] Further on, when the serpent (or his soul) accuses Jung of having 'completely forgotten' who he is, she says that he 'even den[ies] Faust, who walked calmly past all the specters' (*Faust, der an den Spukgeistern ruhigen Ganges vorüberging*) (318).[14] Finally, there is another reference to the figure of Mephistopheles in *Faust* when Jung – somewhat obscurely, it must be admitted – defines Mephistopheles as 'Satan, taken with my serpenthood' (323).

Yet even this quotational mode of relation is complex, not to say complicated. In the chapter entitled 'Nox quarta,' Jung wakes up in a kitchen, in front of the fat cook whom he had met in 'Nox secunda,' and wonders: 'Is this really the realm of the Mothers?' (*ist das wohl das Reich der Mütter?*) (RB: 302). As Shamdasani notes, there is an allusion in these words to the famous Mothers Scene of *Faust*, Part Two, to which Jung had attached great significance in *Symbols and Transformations of the Libido* (1911–12) (RB: 302, note 217). Yet the context – the fat cook with her checkered apron, the curious zoomorphism of 'the gray worm of twilights' with its 'round face' and its laughter, the cook's offer of a glass of water; and the copy of Thomas à Kempis's *The Imitation of Christ*, lying open at the twenty-first chapter – immediately undermines the allusion and 'defamiliarizes' it. Later in the same chapter, in 'the son of the earth' (*der Sohn der Erde*), or 'the dark one whom you should awaken' (RB: 304) – the monstrous creature to whom Jung's soul gives birth in 'The Magician' (RB: 327) – one might hear an allusion to the words of Orestes when he awakes from his seizure in Act 3, Scene 2, of *Iphigenie auf Tauris*.[15]

A fourth mode goes beyond these (sometimes purely) verbal intertextual allusions and consists of specific *themes and motifs* from Goethe's literary repertoire. (Here, as elsewhere, even if the themes are not originally Goethean, Goethe may have likely been responsible for mediating them to Jung.) Under the rubric of such themes and motifs one might include, for example, the shrinking motif – as when Jung, undertaking to cure Izdubar, 'the mighty, the bull-man' (RB: 278), shrinks the god to the size of an egg:

> Yet – a fantasy takes up no space! Why did this excellent thought not occur to me earlier? I return to the garden and with no difficulty squeeze Izdubar into the size of an egg and put him in my pocket.
> (283)

This motif is familiar in German literature: in 'Die neue Melusine,' a novella told in *Wilhelm Meisters Wanderjahre*, for instance, and we also encounter it in the short story analyzed by Aniela Jaffé, E. T. A. Hoffmann's 'The Golden Pot' (Jaffé 1990).

Similarly, the motif of the Kabeiroi – 'elemental spirits, dressed in wrinkled garb, [. . .] dwarfish, shriveled, unspectacular bearers of secret arts, possessors of ridiculous wisdom, first formations of the unformed gold, worms that crawl from the liberated egg of the gods, incipient ones, unborn, still invisible' (RB: 320) – most likely derives from *Symbols and Mythology of the Ancient Peoples* (*Symbolik und Mythologie der alten Völker*) (1810–12) by Friedrich Creuzer (1771–1858) and *On the Deities of Samothrace* (*Über die Gottheiten von Samothrake*) (1815) by Friedrich Wilhelm Joseph Schelling (1775–1854) via Goethe's *Faust*.[16] (Once again, Jung adds his own unique spin: after they have built him a tower, Jung rejects their invitation to become the executioner of his own brain, and turns the sword on the Kabeiroi themselves [RB: 321].)

Equally, a number of motifs are reminiscent of Goethe's 'The Fairy-Tale' (*Das Märchen*), published in 1795: the speaking serpent,[17] the will o' the wisps,[18] and the central symbol of the bridge.[19] In fact, the entire style of *Das Märchen* is eminently comparable to *The Red Book*, which is simply executed on much larger, and much grander, scale. (*Das Märchen* was a text that fascinated Rudolf Steiner, whose own efforts at art and architecture look considerably less eccentric compared with Jung's experiment in *The Red Book*.)[20] Finally, we might ascribe to this mode such specifically Faustian motifs as the theme of becoming (or *Werden*). Exemplified by the entire drama of *Faust* and by the words of the 'Prelude on the Stage,' – 'He who still grows will ever render thanks' (*Ein Werdender wird immer dankbar sein*) (*Faust I*, 1. 183; Goethe 2001: 7) – the theme is reflected in the chapter entitled 'The Magician,' when Jung's serpent (or his soul) asks him whether he has noticed how 'the becoming of the soul follows a serpentine path' (*die Schlangenlinie des seelischen Werdens*) (RB: 317). He later, and 'smilingly,' replies (318): 'The sinuous line of life could not escape me in the long run' (*Des Lebens Schlangenlinie konnte mir auf die Dauer nicht entgehen*) (316).

In *The Red Book*, as in *Faust*, the theme of becoming is related to the experience of hell. A few pages on in 'The Magician,' Jung reflects: 'No one saves us from the evil of becoming, unless we choose to go through Hell' (*Niemand erlöst uns vom Übel des Werdens, es sei denn, dass wir freiwillig durch die Hölle gehen*) (RB: 318). The theme of the descent into hell also underpins both works. In *Faust*, we have a journey into hell: in Part One, into the first *Walpurgisnacht* and into the hell of the seduction and betrayal of Gretchen (involving the murder of her brother, the murder of her mother, and the infanticidal murder of her child), and in Part Two, into the 'classical' *Walpurgisnacht* and into the hellish murder of the innocent old couple, Philemon and Baucis. In *The Red Book*, we enter even more intensely into hell: in *Liber Primus*, Jung undertakes a 'Descent into Hell in the Future' (237); in *Liber Secundus*, he descends again, witnessing in hell the struggle of a maiden with three demons (288–9); in 'The Sacrificial Murder,' Jung is told by his own soul to eat the raw liver of a murdered child – a 'great and dark mystery,' representing Man's 'complicity in the act of evil' (290); and in 'The Magician,' Jung's soul gives birth to a monstrous son, 'a frightful miscreant, a stammerer, a newt's brain, a primordial lizard [. . .] a lazy bug-eyed frog,' because Philemon has deceived Jung, and laid 'a puny basilisk in the nest of the dove,' turning his soul into an 'adulterous whore' and him, Jung, into the 'laughable father of the Antichrist' (327).

One major thematic strand of *Faust*, which resonates in *The Red Book*, is so important that we should consider it as a special (and fifth) mode of relationship: the theme of *magic*. Following the donations from his soul in 'The Three Prophecies' of the misery of war, the darkness of magic, and the gift of religion (RB: 306), Jung undertakes a process of self-vivisection, at the end of which he cuts away his limitation, exposing himself to the multiplicity of the world, which initiates a moment of horror, and provides the motivation for his turn – like Faust – to the second of these gifts, to magic (307).

Now, in *Faust*, magic is a central organizing theme. In the opening scene, 'Night,' of Part One, Faust explains that, dissatisfied with philosophy, law, medicine, and (alas!) theology, he has turned to magic (*Faust*, *Part One*, ll. 377–8; Goethe 1987: 15). Subsequently, we see Faust contemplating the sign of the macrocosm, conjuring up the Earth Spirit (*Erdgeist*), and eventually, as we know, concluding a pact with the devil (see *Faust I*, the scenes 'Night' and 'Faust's Study [II]'; Goethe 1987, 17–19 and 47–56). In Part Two, specific reference is made to magic by Plutus (at the end of the great parade or *Mummenschanz* in Act 1) (*Faust II*, ll. 5985–6; Goethe 1994: 43); by Mephisto (in the scene in the Brightly Lit Hall while Faust descends to the Mothers to recover Helena) (ll. 6315–16; 54); and by the Astrologer (in the subsequent scene, in which Faust conjures up Helena and Paris) (ll. 6391–93; 57). Yet Faust regrets his use of magic, and in the 'Midnight' Scene in Act 5, he renounces its use (ll. 11403–7; 218).

Correspondingly, the theme of magic is explicitly present in *The Red Book*. Two of the chapters of *Liber Secundus* are, as I have already noted, entitled 'The Gift of Magic' and 'The Magician.' In the former, Jung is – like Moses in the Book of Exodus (4: 1–5), or Faust in the Mothers Scene (*Faust II*, ll. 6259–61; Goethe 1994: 52) – presented with a magic rod (RB: 306): he describes it as a 'magical rod' or 'wand' (*Zauberstab*), whose appearance is reminiscent of the gift given to Zarathustra by his disciples in the final chapter of Part One.[21] With his soul (307–8), and then with Philemon (312–14), Jung discusses the function of magic in considerable detail. The tone of the discussion is, by turns, whimsical and gnomic – sometimes both (see RB: 313–14). Yet what magic, as we can see from these passages, involves for Jung, brings us to another (and sixth) mode of relation between *The Red Book* and German classicism, a mode where we encounter a more specific set of *methodological motifs* that move beyond the general consideration of the relation between Art and Nature, that are more than mere throw-away allusions, and that help us to appreciate what is at stake in the theme or motif of magic. Chief among these *methodological motifs* is the theme of *madness* or *folly*.

When the spirit of the times approaches Jung and tells him: 'What you speak, that is madness,' he replies in confirmation: 'It is true, it is true, what I speak is the greatness and intoxication and ugliness of madness' (RB: 230). An important theme in *Liber Primus* is the relation between 'madness' (*Wahnsinn*) and the 'supreme meaning' (*Übersinn*), which is defined as 'the path, the way and the bridge to what is to come' (*die Bahn, der Weg und die Brücke zum Kommenden*) (229). Later, in 'Descent into Hell in the Future,' Jung refers to the ancient topos of 'divine madness': 'Madness is divine' (*Der Wahnsinn ist göttlich*) (238), he tells us.[22] In *Liber Secundus*, in 'Nox secunda,' he returns to this theme: 'The problem of madness is profound' (*Das Problem des Wahnsinns ist tief*) (295), adding: 'Divine madness – a higher form of the irrationality of the life streaming through us – at any rate a madness that cannot be integrated into present-day society – but how?' (*Der göttliche Wahnsinn – eine erhöhte Form der Irrationalität des in uns aufströmenden Lebens – immerhin Wahnsinn, welcher der heutigen Gesellschaft nicht einzugliedern ist – doch wie?*) (295).

In the opening section of 'Nox tertia,' Jung's soul whispers urgently to him:

> Have you recognized your madness and do you admit it? [. . .] Let the light of madness shine, and it will suddenly dawn on you. Madness is not to be despised and not to be feared, but instead you should give it life [*Der Wahnsinn ist nicht zu verachten, sondern du sollst ihm das Leben geben*].
>
> (RB: 298)

While he is in the mental asylum, Jung meets the fool, his neighbor in the next bed, who believes he is Nietzsche and Christ. (Nietzsche was mad, because he came to identify with Christ; this man is *really* mad, because he identifies with Nietzsche *and* Christ.) Finally, in the section entitled 'Trial-by-Examination' (or *Prüfungen*, translated by Kyburz, Peck, and Shamdasani as *Scrutinies*), Jung says: 'I believe that we have the choice: I preferred the living wonders of the god. I daily weigh up my whole life and I continue to regard the fiery brilliance of the god as a higher and fuller life than the ashes of rationality. [*Ich wäge tägliche das Ganze meines Lebens, und noch immer bedeutet mir der Feuerglanz Gottes ein höheres und völligeres Leben als die Asche der Vernünftigkeit*] [. . .] My life wants itself whole [*Mein Leben will sich selbst ganz*]' (RB: 339). This final passage shows, I hope, the ramifications of the topos of divine madness: it takes us to the core of Jung's concerns, both thematic and stylistic, in *The Red Book*, not least the theme of wholeness.

But what has all this to do with Goethe? And with classicism? Surely classicism, in the context of the German eighteenth century, is an embodiment of the Enlightenment virtues of commonsense and rationality? Well, yes and no. When Jung's soul (as a serpent) says to him, 'the living must first begin to live' (*dann müssen doch erst die Lebenden zu leben anfangen*), Jung responds: 'This remark could certainly be deeply meaningful, but it seems to be nothing but a joke' (*diese Bemerkung könnte zwar tiefsinning zu sein, scheint sich aber auf einen Witz zu beschränken*) (RB: 323). And here resides the important point of connection. In his final letter (written to Wilhelm von Humboldt on 17 March 1832), Goethe refers to his *Faust* as *diese sehr ernsten Scherze*, as 'these very serious jokes,' a phrase that exactly captures the complexity of his work (1962–7: 481)[23] – and of *The Red Book*. No one, except perhaps Jung, is more alert than Goethe to the limitations of reason, and hence to the need for what he (and others) term *irony*.

True, in his autobiographical work, *Dichtung und Wahrheit* (1811–14; 1833), Goethe is aware of the dangers of (excessive) irony when he discusses the work of the satirist, Gottlieb Wilhelm Rabener (1714–71) (*Dichtung und Wahrheit*, Part Two, Book Seven, *Werke* [HA]: vol. 9, 261; 1987, 199). But in his 'Preface' to his *Theory of Colours* (*Zur Farbenlehre*) (1810), Goethe is quick to emphasize the *need* for irony (*Farbenlehre*, 'Preface,' *Werke* [HA]: vol. 13, 317; 1970, xli); and in its 'Historical Part,' when he turns to a consideration of his great scientific opponent, Newton, Goethe returns to this theme ('Newtons Persönlichkeit,' *Werke* [HA]: vol. 14, 175). In another late text, a short essay entitled 'Indecision and Surrender' (*Bedenken und Ergebung*) (1820), Goethe addresses himself to the problem of what one might call the 'epistemological gap':

> At this point we encounter a characteristic difficulty – one of which we are not always conscious – namely, that a definite chasm appears to be fixed between idea and experience. Our efforts to overbridge the chasm are forever in vain, but nevertheless we strive eternally to overcome the hiatus with reason, intellect, imagination, faith, emotion, illusion, or – if we are capable of nothing better – with folly.
>
> *Hier treffen wir nun auf die eigene Schwierigkeit, die nicht immer klar ins Bewußtsein tritt, daß zwischen Idee und Erfahrung eine gewisse Kluft befestigt scheint, die zu überschreiten unsere ganze Kraft sich vergeblich bemüht. Demohngeachtet bleibt unser ewiges Bestreben diesen Hiatus mit Vernunft, Verstand, Einbildungskraft, Glauben, Gefühl, Wahn und, wenn wir sonst nichts vermögen, mit Albernheit* [= folly] *zu überwinden.*
> (Naydler 1996: 98; *Werke* [HA]: vol. 13, 31)

In a sense, Jung's experiment in the work on *The Red Book* is the equivalent to Goethe's on optics, inasmuch as both adopt a similar, phenomenological approach. Although it adopts an epic style, *The Red Book* might be thought of as an attempt to produce a kind of *Farbenlehre* of the psyche, inasmuch as it documents and reflects on experience. Moreover, Jung speaks (in the chapter entitled 'The Magician') not just of madness, but of stupidity as a part of magic: 'Stupidity [*das Dumme*] too is part of this, which everyone has a great deal of, and also tastelessness [*Geschmacklosigkeit*], which [for many] is the greatest nuisance' (RB: 314). At this point, in the *Draft*, Jung inserts a lengthy discourse on *stupidity* (315, note 277). It would take us too far away from our discussion to consider Goethe's view (or Schiller's view) of stupidity,[24] but the dialectical relation, as Goethe (and perhaps Jung) understood it, between 'seriousness' and 'jokiness' is captured in the following short poem:

> If I want to take the joke seriously
> Then no one should cry shame on me,
> And if I treat seriousness as a joke,
> Then I still remain the same bloke.
>
> *Wenn ich den Scherz will ernsthaft nehmen,*
> *So soll mich niemand drum beschämen;*
> *Und wenn ich den Ernst will scherzhaft treiben,*
> *So werd ich immer derselbe bleiben.*
>
> (Goethe, 'Sprichwörtlich' 1982: 616)

In short, to understand *The Red Book*, we have to be sensitive, as we do when reading *Faust*, to its use of irony.[25]

With this advice in mind, let us consider the seventh, and final, mode of relation between *The Red Book* and German classicism: its Goethean thematics of *life, the self, death, and beauty*. These themes form such a dense nexus or nucleus, it is difficult to know how to approach them (Jung, too, plainly knew this difficulty: hence the extent and complexity of *The Red Book*). So we can, perhaps, consider these themes under the general rubric of Goethe as a source of *Lebensphilosophie*, and Jung as an adherent of this tradition and as a *Lebensphilosoph*.[26] But what, in this context, do we mean by *life*?

In the first chapter of *Liber Primus*, which bears the programmatic title 'Refinding the Soul,' Jung tells his soul: 'The one thing I have learned is that one must live this life' (*dass man nämlich dieses Leben leben muss*) (RB: 232).[27] In the following chapter, 'Soul and God,' Jung enquires further:

> But how can I attain the knowledge of the heart? You can attain this knowledge only by living your life to the full [*Du kannst dieses Wissen nur dadurch erlangen, dass du dein Leben völlig lebst*] [. . .] It appears as though you want to flee from yourself so as not to have to live what remains unlived until now.
>
> (233)

'But,' he continues, 'you cannot flee from yourself' (*du kannst dir aber nicht entfliehen*) (233–4), citing directly from the opening stanza of Goethe's poem, 'Primal Words. Orphic' (*Urworte. Orphisch*): *So mußt du sein, dir kannst du nicht entfliehen* ('Thus you must be, you cannot flee yourself') (Goethe 1998: 123). Thus the theme of *life* intersects with the theme of *the self.*

Two chapters later in *Liber Primus*, in 'The Desert,' Jung is taken off – in a reprise of another Nietzschean theme[28] – to the desert of the Self:

> My soul leads me into a desert, into the desert of my own self [*in die Wüste meines eigenen Selbst*] [. . .] But I was not my self, confronted with my thoughts. I should also rise up above my thoughts to my own self [*Ich soll auch über meine Gedanken emporsteigen zu meinem eigenen Selbst*].
>
> (RB: 235)

This notion of one's *own self*, or *mein eigener Selbst*, echoes, both verbally and conceptually, what Faust tells us in the famous pact scene of Part One –

> And in my inner self I will sustain
> The experience allotted to the whole
> Race of mankind; my mind shall grasp the heights
> And depths, my heart know all their sorrows and delights.
> Thus I'll expand myself, and their self shall I be,
> And perish in the end, like all humanity.
>
> *Und was der ganzen Menschheit zugeteilt ist,*
> *Will ich in meinem innern Selbst genießen,*
> *Mit meinem Geist das Höchst' und Tiefste greifen,*
> *Ihr Wohl und Weh auf meinen Busen häufen,*
> *Und so mein eigen Selbst zu ihrem Selbst erweitern,*
> *Und, wie sie selbst, am End' auch ich zerscheitern.*
>
> (*Faust I*, ll. 1766–75; Goethe 1987, 54)

– as well as, not coincidentally, being an idea found in Nietzsche, when Zarathustra tells us in 'The Wanderer':

> It is returning, at last it is coming home to me – my own Self and those parts of it that have long been abroad and scattered among all things and accidents. [*Es kehrt nur zurück, es kommt mir endlich heim – mein eigen Selbst, und was von ihm lange in der Fremde war und zerstreut unter alle Dinge und Zufälle.*]
>
> (Nietzsche 1966: 173; 1969: 403)

Jung returns to this theme of the *eigenes* – or as he now calls it, *eigenstes – Selbst* in *Liber Secundus*, in the chapter entitled 'The Sacrificial Murder,' when, toward the end of a page that introduces a remarkable sequence of striking mandalas, he writes: 'But the way is my own self, my own life founded upon myself' (*Der Weg aber ist mein eigenstes Selbst, mein eigenes auf mich gegründetes Leben*) (RB: 291).

To the themes of *life* and *self* at the core of *The Red Book*, we must add a further element: *beauty*. For the 'meaning' of *The Red Book* is tied up with an eminently classical theme: *the quest for beauty*. In 'Descent into Hell in the Future,' Jung – addressing his soul – cries: 'Let me persist in divine astonishment, so that I am ready to behold your wonders' (*Lass mich verharren in göttlicher Fassungslosigkeit, damit ich bereit bin, deine Wunder zu schauen*) (RB: 238). Immediately, Jung links this appeal to the notion of the terror of beauty:[29] 'But who can withstand fear when the divine intoxication and madness comes to him? Love, soul, and God are beautiful and terrible' (*Wer aber könnte, wenn der göttliche Rausch und Wahnsinn ihm ankommt, der Angst widerstehen? Liebe, Seele und Gott sind schön und furchtbar*) (RB: 238). We might compare Jung's (entirely understandable) reaction here with Goethe's various discussions of what it is like when we are confronted with the *Urphänomen* (variously translated as 'primal phenomenon,' 'archetypal phenomenon,' or 'originary phenomenon'): for then, according to Goethe, we experience a kind of anxiety, or even *Angst*. 'The immediate perception of originary phenomena,' he wrote, 'plunges us into a kind of anguish: we sense our inadequacy [. . .]' (Maxims and Reflections, no. 433; Naydler 1996: 108. Translation modified). Or again, 'when archetypal phenomena stand unveiled before our senses, we feel a kind of nervousness, to the point of feeling anguish' (*eine Art von Scheu, bis zur Angst*) (no. 412; 108. Translation modified). Thus it would be no exaggeration to say that, in *The Red Book*, Jung is confronting (and contemplating) the *Urphänomen* of the psyche.

Moreover, the beauty in which Jung is interested is no abstract, intangible, Platonic beauty, but a beauty that is overwhelming, powerful, visceral. Reflecting – after he has met Ammonius, the Libyan anchorite who lives in the desert – on the life of the solitary, Jung remarks: 'The solitary lives in endless desert full of awesome beauty' (*voll schrecklicher Schönheit*), and because 'he looks at the whole and at inner meaning,' because 'he loathes manifold diversity if it is near him,' and because 'he looks at it from afar in its totality,' 'consequently silvery splendor and joy and beauty cloak diversity for him' (RB: 269). And, in turn, Jung reflects: 'You sit and lean against the wall, and look at the beautiful, riddlesome totality' (*das schöne, rätselvolle Ganze*) (270).

Jung's beauty is, so to speak, not very pretty: it is *a beauty beyond the beautiful*. In the chapter entitled 'Death,' Jung interprets his vision in this section of 'the red sun' (RB: 275) – 'a new sun escapes from the bloody sea, and rolls gleamingly toward the utmost depths' (274) – in terms of an unsettling aesthetic: 'blood and murder,' he says, 'have their own peculiar beauty,' and 'one can,' he adds, 'assume the beauty of bloody acts of violence'

(275). And what, at this moment in *The Red Book*, is arising in Jung is not beautiful at all: it is 'the unacceptable, the awfully repulsive,' symbolized by Jung's perishing on a dung heap, surrounded by cackling chickens and being urinated on by a dog (275).[30]

Is this not the same beauty of which Jung speaks when he has opened the egg and found Izdubar transformed into the sun? In 'The Opening of the Egg,' we find a passage emphasizing the intensity – and fragility – of beauty as Jung conceives it: 'I did not know what was happening to me, since simply everything powerful, beautiful, blissful, and superhuman [*alles Mächtige, Schöne, Glückselige, Übermenschliche*] had leaked from my maternal womb; none of the radiant gold remained' (RB: 287). And is not the source of this beauty the essential dualism (ambivalence, ambiguity) of the phenomenal world? In 'The Opening of the Egg,' this is how he describes Nature. The passage reads, in part, like a parody of the famous text 'On Nature,' which is attributed to Goethe (but, in fact, written by Tobler and influenced by Orphic sources) (Goethe 1988: 3–5):[31] '*Nature is playful and terrible.* [. . .] *The way* [. . .] *is both cheerful play and cold horror*' ('Natur ist spielerisch und schrecklich . . . Der Weg . . . ist heiteres Spiel und kaltes Grauen') (RB: 287).

In the final pages of *Scrutinies*, or *Prüfungen*, the theme of beauty returns in the concluding dialogue between ΦΙΛΗΜΩΝ and a blue shadow (which *Black Book* 6 identifies as Christ).[32] ΦΙΛΗΜΩΝ says to Christ (in what is, perhaps, a rerun of the Easter morning scene in the garden between Christ and Mary Magdalene): 'I find you in the garden, beloved. The sins of the world have conferred beauty upon your countenance' (*Die Sünde der Welt hat deinem Antlitz Schönheit gegeben*) (RB: 359). The dualism of ΦΙΛΗΜΩΝ and Baucis (equated here with the Gnostic Simon Magus and Helena of Troy, reincarnated in a prostitute from Tyre) has its counterpart in Christ and his brother, Satan or the 'terrible worm' (RB: 359).[33] Jung's complementaristic (and highly Goethean) point is that one cannot have Heaven without Hell, Christ without Satan, the blue shade without the terrible worm.[34] But if the gift of the worm was 'lamentation and abomination' (*Jammer und Abscheulichkeit*), what the shade brings is beauty – 'I bring you the beauty of suffering' (*die Schönheit des Leidens*) (RB: 359).

Earlier in *Scrutinies* or *Prüfungen*, Jung had undertaken an explicit consideration of a similar theme, tackling the problem of redemption from the viewpoint of aesthetics: 'It appears to me that we benefit in particular from removing every sense of beauty from the thought of redemption' (*Mir scheint, als sei es uns besonders förderlich und sogar nötig, jeden schönen Schein vom Gedanken der Erlösung wegzunehmen*), even if 'a beautiful schimmer spreads out over the thing through the great word,' but 'one can at least doubt whether the work of redemption is in itself a beautiful thing' (*man kann aber mindestens zweifelhaft sein, ob das Erlösungswerk an sich auch eine schöne Sache sei*) (RB: 338). Of course, Jung has a particular example in mind: the Romans 'did not find the hanged Jew exactly tasteful,' nor did 'the gloomy excessive enthusiasm for catacombs' bring with it 'a pleasant shimmer' (*des angenehmen Schimmers*) (338).

Equally, *The Red Book* contains much that is not exactly pleasant – and much that is shocking: the death of the tramp in 'One of the Lowly' (266), or the episode where Jung consumes the murdered child's raw liver (290), or in his reimagining of Elisha's (or Elijah's) resuscitation of a child as an act of necrophilia (304),[35] or in his offer of blood from his heart to the female shadow who gives him the HAP (340). Also disturbing is the identification of Salome, whom Elijah offers to Jung as his wife, with his sister (368 and 249), or Jung's transformations into the *deus leontocephalus*, into 'a laughing being of the forest, a leaf green daimon, a forest goblin and prankster,' and into Odin/Christ (252, 276, and 326). There is the warning about 'the fearful devilishness of human nature' and 'the dreadful worm' with its evil eye, 'awaiting the moment when the beautiful, writhing great with child, seeks to give life to the God' (289), or the fusion of iconography from *Zarathustra* and the Bible in the image when the black serpent enters the body of the crucified and emerges, transformed, from his mouth (309). And yet, over the weeks, months, even years, Jung worked away at the text and illustrations of *The Red Book*, going through draft after draft, buying the parchment and the leather-bound book, giving it a shape, a form, a *Gestalt* – that can only be called aesthetic.

Indeed, perhaps it is only the aesthetic that can cope with the kind of paradox in which Jung was interested. Of these paradoxes at the heart of *The Red Book*, the greatest is surely this: that one of the realities with which one must engage in the course of life is the reality of the end-of-reality, that is to say, *death*. In the chapter in *Liber Primus* entitled 'Death,' Jung tells us that death is something we need: 'Therefore I behold death, since it teaches me how to live. [. . .] Death ripens. [. . .] To be, and to enjoy your being, you need death, and limitation enables you to fulfill your being' (*Um zu sein und deines Seins zu genießen, bedarfst du des Todes, und die Beschränkung bewirkt, dass du dein Sein erfüllen kannst*) (RB: 275). The intensity of language and concentration of expression in these lines is strikingly reminiscent of Rilke, and their message is eminently Goethean: they push to its ultimate existential conclusion the insight expressed by Goethe in the line of one of his poems, that it is in limitation that mastery is to be found (or *in der Beschränkung zeigt sich erst der Meister*) ('Natur und Kunst,' 1983: 164–5; *Werke* [HA]: vol. 1, 245). In 'The Three Prophecies,' Jung alludes to one of the most famous, if ironic, formulations of the idea of mastery-through-limitation in Voltaire's *Candide* (RB: 306).[36] But for Jung, the message of *cultiver notre jardin* is to be taken seriously: 'The future,' he writes, 'should be left to those of the future,' whereas he decides to 'return to the small and the real,' for 'this is the great way' – referring back to the very first chapter title, this is 'the way of what is to come' (306; cf. 229). Thus it is in and through the acceptance of limitation that, both Goethe and Jung suggest, true greatness is to be found; ultimately, that limitation includes death.[37]

In this respect, *The Red Book* fits into the tradition of 'spiritual exercises,' as they have been described by Pierre Hadot, among which one finds the contemplation of death (1995).[38] Death is, then, the 'ultimate reality' with which one has to come to terms, and classicism is, as we have seen, supremely concerned with a coming-to-terms with reality. Another way to describe this process is achieving a sense of solidity (a sense that is so important to Goethe during his visit to Italy), and this search for solidity is bound up with the quest for beauty undertaken by Jung in the experiential production of his *Red Book*.

Perhaps, then, the reason why Jung left *The Red Book* incomplete provides a clue to the meaning of his undertaking in the first place – a clue that points to this work's associations with German classicism, and helps us to appreciate Jung's achievements in *The Red Book* (as well as what are, in his eyes, its failures). In *Memories, Dreams, Reflections*, when *The Red Book* is mentioned, Jung immediately distances himself from it – arguably a strategic move.[39] 'In *The Red Book* I tried an aesthetic elaboration of my fantasies, but never finished,' we read (MDR: 214); in the original German, the emphasis is even stronger, *Ich habe den untauglichen Versuch einer ästhetisierenden Elaboration meiner Phantasien* [. . .] *unternommen* (1990: 191).[40] Why this sense of disappointment, or to put it another way, why did *The Red Book* fail? According to *Memories, Dreams, Reflections*, Jung was not convinced he had found the 'right language,' and he came to eschew his own 'aestheticizing tendency' (*das Ästhetisieren*) (MDR: 213).

Yet although Jung is said to have abandoned his own 'aestheticization' (*das Ästhetisieren*) in favor of the 'understanding' (*das Verstehen*) of 'scientific comprehension' (*das wissenschaftliche Verständnis*), *The Red Book* is a vital residue of what Jung saw as a necessary counterpart of his 'life's work' (MDR: 213). For the 'aestheticizing elaboration' (*die ästhetisierende Elaboration*) involved in its production gave Jung an insight into his 'ethical obligation' toward its images, in a way that, we are told, 'decisively influenced' his conduct of his life (ETG: 192). In this passage, part of which is omitted from *Memories, Dreams, Reflections*, but retained in *Erinnerungen, Träume, Gedanken* (indicated following ¶ below), the argument is thoroughly classical in its embrace of reality, of consciousness, and of life:

> I saw that so much fantasy needed firm ground underfoot, and that I must first return wholly to reality. For me, reality meant scientific comprehension. I had to draw concrete conclusions from the insights the unconscious had given me – and that task was to become a life work.¶
>
> The aestheticizing elaboration in the 'Red Book' was necessary, however much I got annoyed about it; for only through it came the insight into the ethical obligation toward the images. It became clear to me that no language, however perfect it may be, can replace life. If

> it tries to replace life, then not just it, but life itself is ruined. In order to wrest freedom from the tyranny of unconscious presuppositions, one needs both: the realization of both intellectual and ethical obligations.
>
> (MDR: 213; ETG: 192)

The realization of both 'intellectual' and 'ethical' obligations lies in the aesthetic – not, to be sure, simply in the production of pretty things, or even beautiful things, such as elaborately illuminated, lovingly (and calligraphically) transcribed, handsomely leather-bound, big red books, but in life transmuted *through* and *into* the aesthetic that achieves, as Nietzsche put it, the 'aesthetic justification of the world'(1968: *The Birth of Tragedy* §5, §24; 'Attempt at a Self-Criticism' §5), or what one might call (to use a phrase from Jung's *Draft*) 'the art of life.'

We find a similar emphasis to the one in *Memories, Dreams, Reflections* on 'firm ground,' 'concrete conclusions,' and the insight achieved through *The Red Book* that 'no language, however perfect, can replace life,' when, in the chapter entitled 'The Magician,' Jung tells us how he has acquired a kind of 'permanence in change,' or a *Dauer im Wechsel*,[41] which he defines in terms of solidity: 'Thus I built a firm structure. Through this I myself gained stability and duration and could withstand the fluctuations of the personal. Therefore the immortal in me is saved' (*So bildete ich einen festen Bau. Dadurch erlangte ich selber Festigkeit und Dauer und konnte den Schwankungen des Persönlichen widerstehen. Dadurch ist das Unsterbliche an mir gerettet*) (RB: 323). Ultimately, Jung's ambition, like Goethe's, is to achieve a vantage point of stability within a universe of flux and, hence, to attain the kind of happiness expressed in Act 5 of *Faust*, Part Two, by Lynceus the Watchman (who, in turn, is based on a figure in classical literature) –

To seeing born,	*Zum Sehen geboren,*
To scanning called,	*Zum Schauen bestellt,*
To the watchtower sworn,	*Dem Turme geboren,*
I relish the world.	*Gefällt mir die Welt.*
[. . .]	[. . .]
In all I behold	*So seh ich in allen*
Ever-comely design,	*Die ewige Zier,*
As its virtues unfold	*Und wie mir's gefallen,*
I take pleasure in mine.	*Gefall ich auch mir.*
You fortunate eyes,	*Ihr glücklichen Augen,*
All you ever did see,	*Was je ihr gesehn,*
Whatever its guise,	*Es sei, wie es wolle,*
Was so lovely to me!	*Es war doch so schön!*[42]

(*Faust II*, ll. 11288–91, 11296–303; Goethe 2001: 320)

– or, in Jung's words in *The Red Book*, to attain 'the happiness' – or 'the magnificence' – 'of someone who surveys things [. . .] and who lives from himself' (*die Herrlichkeit des Schauenden und des aus sich selber Lebenden*) (RB: 321).

Notes

1 See Jung, *The Red Book: Liber Novus* (2009a) and *Das Rote Buch: Liber Novus* (2009b). Henceforth referred to in parentheses as RB, followed by a page reference. (Although the pagination between the Anglo-American and German editions is not identical, the reference system to the original pages permits one to move between the editions relatively easily.)
2 See also Goethe, *Werke* (1948–60, 1981: vol. 3, 26) (henceforth referred to as *Werke* [HA], followed by volume number and a page reference).
3 Compare with Thomas Mann's remarks about 'the poet (and the philosopher) as a detector, a seismograph, a sensitive medium, without a clear knowledge about this organic function and thus entirely capable of erroneous judgements' (*der Dichter (und der Philosoph) als Melde-Instrument, Seismograph, Medium der Empfindlichkeit, ohne klares Wissen von dieser seiner organischen Funktion und darum verkehrter Urteile nebenher durchaus fähig*) (Mann 1949: 126–7). I am grateful to Malcolm Pender for drawing this passage to my attention and providing the source for it.
4 The publication of *The Red Book* prompts one to ask how the image of the Jung that arises from its illuminated pages may be reconciled with the image of a Jung who held that 'psychology constituted the fundamental scientific discipline, upon which other disciplines should henceforth be based' (Shamdasani 2003: 15).
5 For a discussion of Jung's work as a painter, see Luchsinger (1987: 298–302) and Baumgardt (1987, 303–12). For an insightful analysis of the artistic aspects of *The Red Book*, see Susan Thackrey's contribution in this volume.
6 For a discussion of Jung's 'tower' in Bollingen, see Ziolkowski's 'Carl Gustav Jung: The Tower of the Psyche' (1998: 131–48) and Rosen (1996).
7 See his early poem, 'Gedanken in einer Frühlingsnacht,' discussed in Bishop (2003: 327–43).
8 Compare with William McGuire's observation: '[*The Red Book*] should really form part, sometime, of [Jung's] opus: just as the autobiography is an essential supplement to his other writings, so is the Red Book to the autobiography' (McGuire papers, Library of Congress; cited in Shamdasani, in the 'Introduction' [RB: 221]).
9 Henceforth referred to in parenthesis as MDR, followed by a page reference.
10 Compare with the conceptual unification implicit in the titles – 'Art Forms in Nature,' 'Nature as an Artist' – of the following works by Ernst Haeckel: *Kunstformen der Natur* (1899/1904), and, with Wilhelm Breitenbach, *Natur als Künstlerin; Formenschatz der Schöpfung* (1913). For further discussion of Haeckel's relevance for understanding Jung, see Joe Cambray's contribution in this volume.
11 Jung defines the devil as follows: 'The devil as the adversary is your own other standpoint; he tempts you and sets a stone in your path where you least want it' (RB: 261), and later as 'the sum of the darkness of human nature' (RB: 322).
12 Compare with Nietzsche's *Thus Spoke Zarathustra*: 'Creation – that is the great redemption from suffering, and life's easement' (*Schaffen – das ist die grosse Erlösung vom Leiden, und des Lebens Leichtwerden*) (1969: 111; 1966: 345).
13 See the comments in *Memories, Dreams, Reflections* on Philemon and Baucis in relation to Jung's sense of 'guilt' (MDR: 261).
14 See the 'Midnight' Scene in Act 5 of *Faust, Part Two* (ll. 11407–19; Goethe 1994: 218).

15 ORESTES (recovering from his swoon and standing up)
Give yet another! reach from Lethe's stream
The last reviving draught of cool refreshment!
Soon shall its waters in my bosom still
Life's fitful fever; and my spirit then
Adown oblivion's stream shall glide to you,
Ye spirits shrouded in eternal mist.
With tranquil pleasure in your deep repose,
A weary son of earth may lave his soul! –
What whispering sounds pervade the dreary grove?
What hollow murmurs haunt its twilight gloom? –
They gather round to view the stranger guest!

OREST aus seiner Betäubung erwachend und sich aufrichtend.
Noch einen! reiche mir aus Lethes Fluten
Den letzten kühlen Becher der Erquickung!
Bald ist der Krampf des Lebens aus dem Busen
Hinweggespült; bald fließet still mein Geist,
Der Quelle des Vergessens hingegeben,
Zu euch, ihr Schatten, in die ew'gen Nebel.
Gefällig laßt in eurer Ruhe sich
Den umgetriebnen Sohn der Erde laben! –
Welch ein Gelispel hör' ich in den Zweigen,
Welch ein Geräusch aus jener Dämmrung säuseln? –
Sie kommen schon, den neuen Gast zu sehn!

(Goethe 1882: 51; *Werke* [HA], vol. 5, 41)

For further discussion, see Reuchlein (1983).

16 For the Kabeiroi in *Faust*, see Part Two, the scene 'Rocky Inlets of the Aegean Sea' in the Classical *Walpurgisnacht*, where the mythical sea entities announce the arrival of the Cabiri, dwarf-like divinities of fertility, 'misshapen things' that look like 'dreary pots of clay,' as Homunculus describes them (*Faust II*, ll.8219–20; Goethe 1994: 115). For further discussion, see Kerényi (1941).

17 What does the serpent in *The Red Book* represent? In the chapter entitled 'Mysterium. Encounter,' Jung explains that the serpent represents a 'third principle,' in addition to Elijah (= Logos) and Salome (= Eros) (RB: 246, note 161, cf. Appendix B, 'Commentaries'), defined as 'the earthly essence of man, of which he is not conscious' (RB: 247).

18 For the will o' the wisps, see the following passage:

> Therefore on your journey be sure to take golden cups full of the sweet drink of life, red wine, and give it to dead matter, so that it can win life back. The dead matter will change back into black serpents. Do not be frightened, the serpents will immediately put out the sun of your days, and a night with wonderful will-o'-the-wisps [*mit wunderlichen Irrlichtern*] will come over you.
>
> (RB: 244)

19 For the image of the bridge, see 'But the supreme meaning is the path, the way and the bridge to what is to come. [. . .] The supreme meaning is the beginning and the end. It is the bridge of going across and fulfillment' (RB: 229–30).

20 See Rudolf Steiner's lectures on *Das Märchen* (1904) and (in German) Steiner, 'Goethes geheime Offenbarung: Zu seinem hundertfünfzigsten Geburtstage' (1899) and *Goethes Geistesart in ihrer Offenbarung durch seinen "Faust" und durch "Das Märchen von der Schlange und der Lilie"* (1979: 63–84).

21 Zarathustra's rod is described as 'a staff, upon the golden haft of which a serpent was coiled about a sun' (Nietzsche 1969: 100); Jung's rod is 'a black rod, formed like a serpent – with two pearls as eyes – a gold bangle around its neck' (RB: 307). In his seminar on *Zarathustra*, Jung discussed the symbolism of Zarathustra's staff in some detail (1989: 791–5).

22 See Shamdasani's extensive and informative footnote on this motif (RB: 238, note 89).

23 For further discussion, see Bahr (1972). Similarly, an appreciation of the literary texture of the works of Thomas Mann is impossible without an awareness of irony.

24 Compare with Goethe's poem, *Cophtisches Lied*, 'It is foolish to insist on the improvement of fools!' (*Töricht auf Beßrung der Toren zu harren!*) (Goethe 1982: 293), or Schiller's line, *Mit der Dummheit kämpfen Götter selbst vergebens* ('Even the gods struggle against stupidity in vain') (*Die Jungfrau von Orleans*, Act 3, Scene 6).

25 This vital element of humor is not lost on *The Red Book*'s translators, who write that they 'can imagine Jung laughing' when, in the final section of 'The Psychological Aspects of the Kore,' he presents as an anonymous 'dream-series' twelve episodes from his *Red Book* ('Translators' Note,' RB: 223).

26 On Goethe and *Lebensphilosophie*, see Kern (1942: 75–91); Boss (1942: 75–91); and, more recently, Armstrong (2006).

27 Jung's diction in such passages recalls how Zarathustra addresses (so to speak) parts of himself: to his soul, for instance (as in 'Of the Great Longing'), or (as in 'The Home-Coming') to his solitude (Nietzsche 1966: 238–40, 202–5; 1969: 467–9, 432–5).

28 Compare with the theme of the desert in *Zarathustra:* in 'Of the Three Metamorphoses,' the 'weight-bearing spirit' must hurry into 'the loneliest desert,' while the wanderer (or Zarathustra's shadow) warns, 'Deserts grow: woe to him who harbours deserts!' (*Die Wüste wächst: weh Dem, der Wüsten birgt!*) (Nietzsche 1966: 54 and 316; 1969: 294 and 540).

29 Compare with the famous line in Rilke's first Duino Elegy, *das Schöne ist nichts als des Schrecklichen Anfang* ('Beauty's nothing but beginning of Terror') (1975: 24–5).

30 Compare with the alchemical motif of the dung heap:

> The *lapis philosophorum*, the stone of the greatest price, is at the same time the corner-stone first rejected by the builders; also the matter out of which the stone is made or in which the precious stone is found is what is trodden underfoot or thrown onto dung heaps, cast out in the road. So psychologically it means that the thing which we think the least of, that part of ourselves which we repress perhaps the most, or which we despise, is just the part which contains the mystery.
>
> (Jung 1989: 953)

31 For further discussion of this text, see Schulz (1938: 79–100), Dornseiff (1939 274–6), Kistler (1954: 383–9), Hermann (1974: 77–100), and Fullenwider (1986: 170–7).

32 On the 'blue midday spectre' and ΦΙΛΗΜΩΝ's 'midday guest,' see 'The Magician' (RB: 316).

33 Compare with Jung's later discussion of Christ and Satan as 'brothers' in *Answer to Job* (1952/1969: CW 11 §649–§654).

34 Compare with Goethe's comments in his tribute to Shakespeare (1771), where he suggested that 'what noble philosophers have said about the world applies to Shakespeare too – 'What we call evil is only the other side of good; evil is necessary for good to exist and is part of the whole, just as the tropics must be torrid and Lapland frigid for there to be a temperate zone' (1986: 165) – and in his review of Sulzer's *Fine Arts* in 1772, where he stated that, in nature, 'beautiful and ugly, good and evil, all

exist side by side with equal rights' (*Werke* [HA]: vol. 12, 18). For further discussion, see Hentschel (1940: 21).

35 See 1 Kings 17:17–24, where Elijah resuscitates the son of a widow, and 2 Kings 4:8–37, where Elisha restores to life the son of a Shunammite.

36 For further discussion, see John Beebe's contribution to this volume.

37 Cf. Jung's comment, 'Life and death must strike a balance in your existence' (*Leben und Tod müssen sich in deinem Dasein die Waage halten*) (RB: 274), and the addition in his *Draft:* 'To live what is right and to let what is false die, that is the art of life' (*Das Richtige leben und das Unrichtige sterben zu lassen, das ist die Kunst des Lebens*) (274, note 75).

38 Interestingly, it has also been suggested that, for Jung, analysis was a modern form of the *ars moriendi* (Shamdasani 2008: 24).

39 Compare with R. F. C. Hull's reaction to *The Red Book:* '[Aniela Jaffé] showed us the famous Red Book, full of real mad drawings with commentaries in monkish script; I'm not surprised Jung keeps it under lock and key! [. . .] The Red Book made a profound impression on me; there can be no doubt that Jung has gone through everything that an insane person goes through, and more. Talk about Freud's self-analysis: Jung is a walking asylum in himself!' (McGuire papers, Library of Congress; cited by Shamdasani, 'Introduction,' RB: 221).

40 Henceforth referred to as ETG, followed by a page reference.

41 See Goethe's poem of this title in *Selected Poems* (1983: 84–6; *Werke* [HA]: vol. 1, 247). In a marginal note in his Red Book, Jung cites a phrase from J. J. Manget's *Bibliotheca chemica curiosa, seu rerum ad alchemiam pertinentium thesaurus instructissimis* (1702), *accipe quod tecum ist* ('accept what is present') (RB: 321, note 314).

42 Compare with the figure of the watchman on the roof in *Agamemnon*, the first part of Aeschylus's trilogy *The Oresteia* (Knox 1993: 305–6).

References

Armstrong, J. (2006) *Love, Life, Goethe: How to be Happy in an Imperfect World*, London: Allen Lane.

Bahr, E. (1972) *Die Ironie im Spätwerk Goethes: ". . . diese sehr ernsten Scherze. . .,"* Berlin: Erich Schmidt Verlag.

Baumgardt, U. (1987) 'Betrachtung eines Bildes von C. G. Jung,' *Analytische Psychologie*, 18 (1987): 303–12.

Bishop, P. (2003) 'C. G. Jung and "Naturmystik": The Early Poem "Gedanken in einer Frühlingsnacht," *German Life and Letters*, 56:4 (October): 327–43.

Boss, A. (1942) 'Goethes Begriff des Schauens', in H. Kern, *Von Paracelsus bis Klages: Studien zur Philosophie des Lebens*, 75–91, Berlin: Widukind.

Carotenuto, A. (1982) *A Secret Symmetry: Sabina Spielrein Between Jung and Freud*, trans. A. Pomerans, J. Shepley, and K. Winston, New York: Pantheon Books.

Dornseiff, F. (1939) 'Die antike Quelle von Goethe-Tobler's Aufsatz "Die Natur,"' *Die Antike*, 15: 274–6.

Fullenwider, H. F. (1986) 'The Goethean Fragment "Die Natur" in English translation,' *Comparative Literature Studies*, 23: 170–7.

Goethe, J. W. von (1882) *The Dramatic Works of Goethe*, trans. W. Scott, E. A. Bowring, and A. Swanwick, New York: Lovell, Coryell.

—— (1948–60) *Werke*, ed. E. Trunz [Hamburger: Ausgabe], 14 vols, Hamburg: Wegner. Reprinted in 1981 by Munich: Beck.

—— (1962–7) *Briefe* [Hamburger Ausgabe], ed. K. R. Mandelkow, 4 vols, Hamburg: Wegner.
—— (1970) *Theory of Colours*, trans. C. Lock Eastlake [1840], Cambridge, MA, and London: MIT Press.
—— (1982) *Gedichte in zeitlicher Folge*, ed. H. Nicolai, Frankfurt am Main: Insel.
—— (1983) *Selected Poems*, ed. C. Middleton [Goethe Edition, vol. 1], Boston, MA: Suhrkamp/Insel Publishers.
—— (1986) *Essays on Art and Literature*, ed. J. Gearey, trans. E. von Nardroff and E. H. von Nardroff [Goethe Edition, vol. 3], New York: Suhrkamp Publishers.
—— (1987a) *Faust: Part One*, trans. D. Luke, Oxford and New York: Oxford University Press.
—— (1987b) *From My Life: Poetry and Truth: Parts One to Three*, eds T. P. Saine and J. L. Sammons, trans. R. R. Heitner [Goethe Edition, vol. 4], New York: Suhrkamp Publishers.
—— (1988) 'On Nature,' in *Scientific Studies*, ed. and trans. D. Miller [Goethe Edition, vol. 12], New York: Suhrkamp Publishers.
—— (1994) *Faust: Part Two*, trans. D. Luke, Oxford and New York: Oxford University Press.
—— (2001) *Faust*, ed. C. Hamlin, trans. W. Arndt, 2nd edn, New York and London: Norton.
Hadot, P. (1995) *Philosophy as a Way of Life: Spiritual Exercises from Socrates to Foucault*, ed. A. I. Davidson, trans. M. Chase, Oxford: Blackwell.
Haeckel, E. (1899/1904) *Kunstformen der Natur*, Leipzig: Verlag des Bibliographischen Instituts.
Haeckel, E., and W. Breitenbach (1913) *Natur als Künstlerin; Formenschatz der Schöpfung*, Berlin: Vita.
Henderson, R. (2009) '*The Red Book – Prima materia* of C. G. Jung: An "Enterview" with Sonu Shamdasani,' *Spring*, 32: 185–91.
Hentschel, C. (1940) *The Byronic Teuton: Aspects of German Pessimism 1800–1933*, London: Methuen.
Hermann, I. (1974) 'Goethes Aufsatz *Die Natur* und Freuds weitere philosophisch-psychologische Lektüre aus den Jahren 1880–1900,' *Jahrbuch der Psychoanalyse*, 7: 77–100.
Horton, S. (2009) 'Inside Jung's *Red Book*: Six questions for Sonu Shamdasani,' *Harpers*, October 2009. Available online at http://www.harpers.org/archive/2009/10/hbc-90005940 (accessed 15 January 2010).
Jaffé, A. (1990) *Bilder und Symbole aus E.T.A. Hoffmanns Märchen "Der goldne Topf"* 1986], Zurich: Daimon.
Jung, C. G. (1952/1969) 'Answer to Job,' in *Psychology and Religion: West and East, The Collected Works of C. G. Jung*, vol. 11, Princeton: Princeton University Press.
—— (1983) *Memories, Dreams, Reflections: Recorded and edited by Aniela Jaffé*, trans. R. and C. Winston, London: Fontana.
—— (1989) *Nietzsche's 'Zarathustra': Notes of the Seminar Given in 1934–1939*, ed. J. L. Jarrett, 2 vols, London: Routledge.
—— (1990) *Erinnerungen, Träume, Gedanken von C. G. Jung: Aufgezeichnet und herausgegeben von Aniela Jaffé*, Olten and Freiburg im Breisgau: Walter.
—— (2009a) *The Red Book: Liber Novus*, ed. S. Shamdasani, trans. M. Kyburz, J. Peck, and S. Shamdasani, New York and London: Norton.

—— (2009b) *Das Rote Buch: Liber Novus*, ed. S. Shamdasani, Düsseldorf: Patmos.

Kerényi, K. (1941) *Das Aegäische Fest: Die Meergötterszene in Goethes "Faust II,"* Amsterdam: Pantheon.

Kerr, J. (1994) *A Most Dangerous Method: The Story of Jung, Freud, and Sabina Spielrein*, London: Sinclair-Stevenson.

Kistler, M. O. (1954) 'The Sources of the Goethe–Tobler Fragment "Die Natur,"' *Monatshefte*, 46: 383–9.

Knox, B. (ed.) (1993) *The Norton Book of Classical Literature*, New York and London: Norton.

Luchsinger, K. (1987) 'Ein unveröffentlichtes Bild von C.G. Jung: "Landschaft mit Nebelmeer,"' *Analytische Psychologie*, 18: 298–302.

Mann, T. (1949) *Die Entstehung des Doktor Faustus: Roman eines Romans*, Amsterdam: Bermann-Fischer.

Mallarmé, S. (1945) 'Le Livre, instrument spiritual,' in *Œuvres complètes*, 382–7, Paris: Gallimard.

Naydler, J. (ed.) (1996) *Goethe on Science: A Selection of Goethe's Writings*, Edinburgh: Floris Books.

Nietzsche, F. (1966) *Werke in drei Bänden*, ed. K. Schlechta, vol. 2, Munich: Hanser.

—— (1968) *The Birth of Tragedy* and 'Attempt at a Self-Criticism,' *Basic Writings*, ed. and trans. W. Kaufmann, New York: Modern Library.

—— (1969) *Thus Spoke Zarathustra*, trans. R. J. Hollingdale, Harmondsworth: Penguin.

Philemon Foundation (2009) 'Publication of *The Red Book*,' Press release, April 2009.

Reuchlein, G. (1983) *Die Heilung des Wahnsinns bei Goethe: Orest, Lila, der Harfner und Sperata*, Frankfurt: Lang.

Rilke, R. M. (1975) *Duino Elegies*, trans. J. B. Leishman and S. Spender, London: Chatto & Windus.

Rosen, D. (1996) *The Tao of Jung: The Way of Integrity*, New York: Viking Arkana.

Schulz, F. (1938) 'Der pseudogoethische Hymnus an die Natur,' in H. Cysarz et al., *Internationale Forschungen zur deutschen Literaturgeschichte: Julius Petersen zum 60. Geburtstag dargebracht*, 79–100, Leipzig: Quelle & Meyer.

Shamdasani, S. (1992) 'Memories, Dreams, Omissions,' *Spring: A Journal of Archetype and Culture*, 38: 115–37.

—— (2003) *Jung and the Making of a Modern Psychology: The Dream of a Science*, Cambridge: Cambridge University Press.

—— (2008) '"The Boundless Expanse": Jung's Reflections on Life and Death,' *Quadrant: Journal of the C. G. Jung Foundation for Analytical Psychology*, 38: 9–32.

Steiner, R. (1899) 'Goethes geheime Offenbarung: Zu seinem hundertfünfzigsten Geburtstage,' *Magazin für Literatur*, 68:34 (August 1899). Available online at http://www.anthroposophie.net/steiner/bib_steiner_goethes_geheime-offenbarung.htm (accessed 18 August 2007).

—— (1904) Lectures on *Das Märchen* on 4 April and 27 November 1904. Available online at http://wn.rsarchive.org/Lectures/SerpLily/19040404p01.html and http://wn.rsarchive.org/Lectures/SerpLily/19041127p01.html (accessed 18 February 2009).

—— (1979) *Goethes Geistesart in ihrer Offenbarung durch seinen "Faust" und durch "Das Märchen von der Schlange und der Lilie,"* Dornach/Schweiz: Rudolf Steiner Verlag.

Stephenson, R. H. (2010) *Studies in Weimar Classicism: Writing as Symbolic Form*, Oxford, Bern, Berlin: Lang.

Stokes, A. (1947) *Inside Out: An Essay in the Psychology and Aesthetic Appeal of Space*, Harmondsworth: Penguin.
Ziolkowski, T. (1998) 'Carl Gustav Jung: The Tower of the Psyche,' in *The View from the Tower: Origins of an Antimodernist Image*, 131–48, Princeton: Princeton University Press.

3

THE RED BOOK

Entrances and exits

Joseph Cambray

October 2009 saw the highly successful launch of Carl Gustav Jung's previously unpublished narratives and images of a set of transformative inner experiences known as *The Red Book* at the Rubin Museum in New York; to accompany this exhibit, the original, bound manuscript was on display. The original then traveled to Los Angeles to the Hammer Museum, and in June 2010 to a show at the Library of Congress where a symposium in honor of C. G. Jung and *The Red Book* was held in conjunction with the opening of the exhibit. In December 2010 the book returned to Zürich where it was exhibited at the Rietberg Museum. There seems to be a sense of *kairos* about this enterprise, what I would call a 'moment of complexity,' borrowing the term from Mark C. Taylor (2001). A complex and multilayered literary construction, recording Jung's visions transcribed in gothic script and illuminated as a medieval manuscript with additional artistic images, *The Red Book* holds much of the experiential background to Jung's later theoretical and clinical writings.

One of Jung's signature concepts is the archetype. While his conceptual formulations began in 1912, it was not until 1919 that Jung first used the term *archetype* (in the essay 'Instinct and the Unconscious,' 1919/1960), shortly after he finished writing the material that would form the text of *The Red Book*. In succeeding years, he went on to differentiate the archetype as a virtual pattern (the so-called *archetype-an-sich*) from its content (archetypal imagery). He did this in part to avoid a Lamarckian reading of archetypes. However, Jung was not always consistent or clear about these distinctions; for example, during a 1938 seminar, *Children's Dreams*, in addressing archetypal content, he said, 'The archetype . . . is capable of reproducing again exactly the same images in an identical way' (2008: 16). Even late in life, in a letter written on the 14 June 1958 to Michael Fordham, Jung still mused about the possibility of inherited archetypal images:

> I don't flatter myself on having a theory of heredity. I share the ordinary views about it. I am convinced that individual acquisitions

> under experimental conditions are not inherited. I don't believe that this statement could be generalized, since changes in individual cases must have been inherited, otherwise no change would have come about in phylogenesis; or we would be forced to assume that a new variety, or a new species, was shaped by the creator on the spot without inheritance . . . For our purposes it is highly indifferent whether archetypes are handed down by tradition and migration or by inheritance . . . The assumption, therefore, that the (psychoid) archetypes are inherited is for many reasons far more probable than that they are handed down by tradition.
>
> (1975: 450)

By examining some personal details from Jung's adolescence, as recorded in his biographical statement *Memories, Dreams, Reflections* (1963), in conjunction with *The Red Book*, the influence of Ernst Haeckel, the great nineteenth-century German evolutionist, will also become apparent.

Early in *The Red Book*, in the section titled 'On the Service of the Soul' in *Liber Primus*, Jung writes, in response to a directive from the spirit of the depths, all the dreams he can recall (2009: 234). In footnote 64, Sonu Shamdasani notes that Jung wrote down two pivotal dreams in his *Black Book #2* (the *Black Books* contain the original manuscript texts from which *The Red Book* was constructed). These dreams date from the time he was 19 years old and was wrestling with which direction to go in life – toward the sciences or the humanities. Thus, the dreams are Jung's recollection, in November 1913, of dreams he presumably had in 1894. From *Memories, Dreams, Reflections*, we know the specific dreams. Here is the first:

> I was in a dark wood that stretched along the Rhine. I came to a little hill, a burial mound, and began to dig. After a while I turned up, to my astonishment, some bones of prehistoric animals. This interested me enormously, and at that moment I knew: I must get to know nature, the world in which we live, and the things around us.
>
> (1963: 85)

Then the second dream:

> I was in a wood; it was threaded with watercourses, and in the darkest place I saw a circular pool, surrounded by dense undergrowth. Half immersed in the water lay the strangest and most wonderful creature: a *round animal, shimmering in opalescent hues, and consisting of innumerable little cells, or of organs shaped like tentacles. It was a giant radiolarian*, measuring about three feet across. It seemed to me indescribably wonderful that this magnificent creature should be lying there undisturbed, in the hidden place, in the clear, deep water.

> It aroused in me an intense desire for knowledge, so that I awoke with a beating heart.
>
> (85, emphasis mine)

Jung goes on to say: 'These two dreams decided me overwhelmingly in favor of science, and removed all my doubts' (85).

It is not clear whether Jung recorded the dreams at age 19, but it was 19 years later that he recalled this material. The reader is left uncertain as to the accuracy of the images of these dreams, and given the highly charged emotional state Jung was in at the start of writing *The Red Book*, there may be nuances that the 38-year-old Jung includes that add to his sense of certainty. Be that as it may, what strikes me as most curious for a medical man, well trained in biology, is Jung's conflation of species, in particular *radiolarians* and *medusae* (jelly fish). Radiolarians are single-cell creatures (plankton) with fantastic exoskeletons; they don't have 'tentacles,' but multicellular medusae, which can easily reach three feet in diameter, do have them. At the time Jung had these dreams, however, there were some remarkable images at the interface of art and science in popular culture. The most striking of these images came from Ernst Haeckel.

Haeckel had begun publishing remarkable renditions of radiolarians from microscopic identifications as early as 1862 as part of his work as a marine biologist. His most striking artistic works were published in a set of ten folios between 1899 and 1904, culminating in a beautifully illustrated book, *Kunstformen der Natur/Art Forms in Nature* (1904/1998), which contains numerous images of both radiolarians and medusae among other creatures. A sample from the book along with some electron micrographs of radiolarians are shown in Plate 1 along with an example of his *Discomedusae* and a contemporary photograph (Plate 2). The mandalic qualities of Haeckel's drawings associated with oceanic depths are unmistakable, as is his personal and libidinal investment in the images (see Plate 2 for the medusa he named after his first wife, Anna Sethe). No doubt Jung would have seen such images, not only in medical school but also in various places throughout culture. His psyche, both at age 19 and again in 1913 at age 38, had certainly incorporated these images into his dreams and fantasies.

The impact of Haeckel's 'scientific art' on the culture of the times is well known. Haeckel's imagery influenced the *Jugendstil* (youth style) movement in German-speaking cultures as well as its better known international counterpart, Art Nouveau, which held sway from about 1890 to 1914. René Binet's entrance to the Paris World Exposition in 1900 was directly modeled on Haeckel's drawings of radiolarians. His influence on Hermann Obrist, Alfonse Mucha, Edvard Munch, Franz Marc, Paul Klee, Wassily Kandinsky, Paul Gauguin, Henri Matisse, and Berlin Dada have been well documented (see Morton 2009); Isadora Duncan was another great fan of his. Thus, it is not surprising that some of his imagery would have impacted the youthful

C. G. Jung's imagination. However, it may be productive to look a bit deeper into Haeckel's influence on Jung.

Ernst Heinrich Philipp August Haeckel (1834–1919)

One of the most eminent nineteenth-century German biologists, Haeckel was also a zoologist, physician, philosopher, naturalist, and an artist. Although trained as a physician, Haeckel abandoned his practice in 1859 after reading Charles Darwin's *On the Origin of Species*. Instead, he became a professor of comparative anatomy at the University of Jena. In the late eighteenth and early nineteenth centuries, Jena had emerged as one of the leading universities in Germany with a faculty that included Friedrich Shiller, Johann Gottlieb Fichte, G. W. F. Hegel, F. W. J. Schelling, and Friedrich von Schlegel; Goethe also spent nearly five years in Jena, due to his friendship with Schiller, which had developed at the University. The University had been at the center of the emergence of German idealism and early Romanticism and Haeckel was steeped in these views

Haeckel discovered, described, and named thousands of new species, mapped genealogical trees relating all life forms, and coined many terms in biology, including *phylum, phylogeny,* and *ecology.* His first great publication was the *Monograph on Radiolarians* in 1862, which remained a key text in the field until about 30 years ago. His evolutionary biology combined elements from Darwin, Lamarck, and Goethe, to which he sometimes added his own intuitions, moving beyond the evidence available at the time. A telling example of his intuitive approach was his prediction, following Darwin's first publications, that ancestral human remains would be found in the Dutch East Indies. Inspired by these speculations, Eugene Dubois, a student of Max Fübringer – himself a student of Haeckel's – in fact discovered remains that fit Haeckel's prediction. Although Haeckel had proposed that this ancestral species be named *Pithecanthropus alalus*, it has come to be known today as *Homo erectus* (Richards 2008).

Haeckel's influence on Jung

Haeckel promoted and popularized Charles Darwin's writings in Germany; he also developed the controversial recapitulation theory, or 'biogenetic law' – 'ontogeny recapitulates phylogeny' – claiming that an individual organism's biological development, or ontogeny, parallels and summarizes its species' evolutionary development, or phylogeny. He was one of the first to consider psychology as a branch of physiology and thought there was a psychological aspect to his recapitulation theory. His views are now termed the 'strong' recapitulation hypothesis, as it portrays ontogeny as repeating forms of adult ancestors, whereas an alternative, 'weak' recapitulation hypothesis postulates that what is repeated (and built on) is the ancestral embryonic development process. In the weak model, organ recapitulation is disambiguated from the notion of the whole organism being recapitulated, which is closer to contemporary views. Haeckel supported his theory with embryo drawings that have since been shown to be oversimplified and, in part, inaccurate; the theory is now considered a gross oversimplification of quite complicated relationships. This becomes relevant in Plate 3, where a nineteenth-century chart of the early phases of cell proliferation in embryological development that Haeckel used in teaching is placed alongside page 32 of *Liber Secundus.* In a note, Sonu Shamdasani makes a comparison of the image on page 32 with the mosaics at Ravenna, suggesting they are a prime source for the image (2009: 275, note 81). Although this is likely accurate, I also think that Haeckel's imagery serves as an important second source. The homunculus-like figures in the 'egg' of Jung's image could be taken to imply a sort of psychic recapitualationism. There are also other images (see, for example, page 79) in *The Red Book* that reflect this parallel with early embryology.

That Jung would have employed Haeckel's biogenetic law was not unusual for the times. Freud, as well as many other psychologists of the era, also embraced the concept. In his 1916 *Introductory Lectures on Psychoanalysis,* Freud posits, 'Each individual somehow recapitulates in an abbreviated form the entire development of the human race' (1916/1963: 199; quoted in Gould 1977: 156). And in the 1914 preface to the third edition of the *Three Essays on the Theory of Sexuality,* he notes, 'The phylogenetic disposition can be seen at work behind the ontogenetic process' (1905: xvi; quoted in Gould 1977: 156). By the time Freud wrote *Totem and Taboo,* he had made mental recapitulation into a cornerstone of his theory of neurosis. In a letter to Sandor Ferenczi on 12 July 1915, while in the process of preparing the 'Overview of the Transference Neuroses,' Freud sets out

> a series of chronological starting points in individual cases of illness which runs as follows: Anxiety hysteria – conversion hysteria – obsessional neurosis – dementia praecox – paranoia – melancholia – mania . . . what are now neuroses were once phases of the human condition.
>
> (Letter 551 in Freud and Ferenczi 1996: 65–6)

In his view, 'modern savages' function at levels comparable to 'civilized children.'

Jung likewise embraced strong recapitulationist views throughout his career; for example, in 'On the Psychology of the Unconscious' in 1912, he writes:

> our knowledge of comparative anatomy and the history of development, which show us how the structure and function of the human body are the results of a series of embryonic changes . . . correspond

> to similar changes in the history of the race. Therefore, the supposition is justified that ontogenesis corresponds in psychology to phylogenesis. Consequently, it would be true, as well, that the state of infantile thinking in the child's psychic life, as well as in dreams, is nothing but a re-echo of the prehistoric and ancient.
>
> (1916/1969: 28; quoted in Gould 1977: 161)

Then, in 1928, writing in English on 'Child Development and Education,' he comments:

> [The] possibility of regression to the primitive stage is explained by the fundamental biogenetic law which holds good not only for the development of the body, but also in all probability for that of the psyche.
>
> According to this law the evolution of the species repeats itself in the embryonic development of the individual. Thus, to a certain degree, man in his embryonic life passes through the anatomical forms of primeval times. If the same law holds for the mental development of mankind, it follows that the child develops out of an originally unconscious, animal condition into consciousness, primitive at first, and then slowly becoming more civilized.
>
> (Jung 1928/1954: par. 104–5)

And still later in 1946, long after the biogenetic law had lost support in the biological sciences, Jung states in 'The Gifted Child':

> Childhood, however, is a state of the past. Just as the developing embryo recapitulates, in a sense, our phylogenetic history, so the child-psyche relives 'the lesson of earlier humanity' as Nietzsche called it.

He continues on to link this with archetypal theory: 'Knowledge of the universal origins builds the bridge between the lost and abandoned world of the past and the still larger inconceivable world of the future.'(1946/1954: par. 250)

However, as the renowned paleontologist and evolutionary biologist Stephen Jay Gould, drawing on an unpublished thesis by R. McCormick, has pointed out:

> Yet, even though Jung spoke more elegantly than Freud of his belief in recapitulation, Jung's approach to psychoanalysis guaranteed that he would not make much use of Haeckel's doctrine within his system. The child, to be sure, recapitulates his past in proper phyletic sequence – but this has little relevance to the study and cure of adult

> neuroses. A child usually develops few psychological problems during the period of his recapitulation. He is dominated by instincts and does not understand the significance of the archetypes he is experiencing. Libido is not exclusively sexual and the causes of neurosis do not lie in the events of childhood; neuroses do not represent a fixation of sexual energy at an infantile (= ancestral) stage that should be repressed and superseded in normal development.
>
> Return, then, to Freud's metaphor for the mind – Rome with all its buildings intact. For Jung, only this adult arrangement matters. . . . The adult mind contains an entire history of its past as racial memory in a collective unconscious. Jung's concept is static: knowing the ontogenetic order of racial memories does not facilitate the study and cure of neuroses. . . . Neuroses are not infantile stages representing a definite time of ancestral history, but events of the moment that call forth images from a collective unconscious. Jung's appeal is not to recapitulation (an ontogenetically ordered series of ancestral stages), but to a general notion of racial memory (the static possession by adults of a complete racial history). . . . Recapitulation ceases to be a question of research for Jung because the archetypes exist independently of any individual's development.
>
> (1977: 162–3)

Daniel Schacter in his study of Richard Semon, *Forgotten Ideas, Neglected Pioneers*, feels Jung is not to be included as a memory–heredity theorist because he 'had almost nothing to say about heredity (or Lamarckism) and viewed archetypes as part of the basic *structure* of the psyche rather than as inherited "racial memories"' (2001: 107, note 8). However, he is basing this in large part on the writings of Jolande Jacobi (1959), whose interpretation of Jung's theories minimizes the inheritance of images in contradistinction to some of the quotes already presented.

Jung did not uniformly embrace Haeckel's ideas and is even known to have been critical of him. Wolfgang Giegerich in *Spring* presents an argument for the difference between Erich Neumann's embrace of Haeckel's law compared with Jung's discomfort with it (1975). Shamdasani, however, demonstrates that Jung initially endorsed Neumann's views and that it was Michael Fordham who educated Jung on the problems with the biogenetic law (2003: 267).[1] Questions have also been raised about Jung's relations to Haeckel's ideas on monism. Jung is known to have written letters of protest to the *Neue Zürcher Zeitung* in January 1912 about a lecture attacking psychoanalysis, which was given at the Kepler-Bund (an organization directly antithetical to Haeckel's Monisten-Bund) in Zürich. At the time, opposition to psychoanalysis and Haeckel's Monisten-Bund, a scientifically oriented group opposed to dogmatic religion, were closely linked (Ellenberger 1970: 810–15). In 1910, Jung had previously expressed concern about the Monisten-Bund to

Freud for its inclusion of nonprofessionals (McGuire 1974: letter 217J). Furthermore, Giegerich claims with some justification that Jung should be read as a Platonic dualist. Thus, Jung was, at best, overtly ambivalent about Haeckel's influence.[2]

Jung's views on racial memory and the archeological layering of the collective unconscious, with their Haeckelian overtones, could also be revisited in terms of contemporary biological studies on the relationship between the development of the organism and its phylogenetic history, including some reassessments and revaluation of aspects of Haeckel's work and ideas. Evolutionary development (at times called 'Evo-Devo') is a burgeoning new field, barely 10 years old, that reexamines the relationship between ontogeny and phylogeny, including the recent research reviving interest in *epigenesis* (the theory postulating that an individual develops by successive differentiation of an unstructured egg rather than by a simple enlarging of a preformed entity[3]). Epigenetics serves to bridge genotype and phenotype. More technically, according to Aaron Goldberg and colleagues, 'Epigenetics may be defined as the study of any potentially stable and, ideally, heritable change in gene expression or cellular phenotype that occurs without changes in Watson-Crick base-pairing of DNA' (2007). Epigenetic mechanisms regulate gene expression but do not involve alterations in the genetic code itself. Likewise, epigenetic modifications can abolish gene function, even without a DNA sequence change. A reexamination of archetypal theory based on these ideas has begun but will require much more exploration, especially as the field itself is expanding rapidly; this area is just one potential place of new meaning for Jungian scholars that could emerge from study of *The Red Book*. As further support of Jung's borrowings and incorporations of Haeckel, I return to a set of images and, hence, ideas in *The Red Book*.

Haeckel's influence on the 'mandala' series of *The Red Book*

As noted, Plate 3 has potential as an image of incubation. Following from this, I proceed to the 'mandala' series in *The Red Book* (2009: 80–9). Plate 4 compares one of Haeckel's *Discomedusae* images with the first image in the series, which is found on page 80. We know from Appendix A that the pencil sketch for this was done on 2 August 1917. According to Shamdasani, this was during the period '[b]etween June 11 and October 2, 1917, [when] Jung was on military service in Chateau d'Oex, as commander of the English prisoners of war' (206).[4] The sketch is entitled 'Phanes' and has a legend at the bottom, 'metabolism in the individual.' In Orphic cosmogony, Phanes was the primeval procreative force, the generator of new life. He was hatched from the world egg (the primordial mixture of elements) when it was broken open by Kronos and Ananke.

Returning to the mandala series, the next image in *The Red Book* shifts focus inward onto the fourfold form around a central 'seed' pocket, which is beginning to undergo a transformation (Jung 2009: 81). The form has some obvious similarities to select aspects of Haeckel's medusae with their fourfold radial symmetry, especially when seen from below – note the center of the medusa's form is where the mouth, anus, and gonads (*v.i.*) are located, that is, where its metabolism begins and ends. This is not to equate Jung's images with Haeckel's engravings but to suggest that Jung had a sense of the same mythic quality that lay behind Haeckel's images, recognizing why they were so mesmerizing to the culture of that period. Jung seems to be incorporating them into his own psychological phylogeny, the collective unconscious.

In the next picture, Jung has returned to a fully circular mandala with increased complexity in the figure's symmetry (2009: 82). Compare this to engravings by Haeckel of creatures with highly ordered, symmetric features, such as *Diatomea* (Haeckel 1904/1998: Plates 4 and 84) and *Echinidea* (Plate 60), among others with the radial, star-burst symmetry. Again from Appendix A of *The Red Book* we know Jung made an initial drawing on 4 and 7 August (2009: 361).

During this time, Jung was struggling with imaginings about being an artist, not unlike Haeckel (1963). An inner feminine voice, which Jung recognized as that of a patient, whom Shamdasani has identified as Maria Moltzer, claimed 'That is art.' Jung vigorously disagreed (1963: 185–6). He expressed his distrust of this voice, labeling the patient 'a talented psychopath.' This issue came to a head when he was at Chateau d'Oex:

> One day . . . I received a letter from that esthetic lady in which she again stubbornly maintained that the fantasies arising from my unconscious had artistic value and should be considered art. The letter got on my nerves. It was far from stupid, and therefore dangerously persuasive.
>
> (195)

He discusses some of his internal struggle with her letter and then notes, 'Out of this irritation and disharmony within myself there proceeded, the following day, a changed mandala: part of the periphery had burst open and the symmetry was destroyed' (195; *The Red Book*, Appendix A, shows this sketch and the date [2009: 361]).

Plate 5 shows pages 83 and 84 of *The Red Book*, in which something dark is rising from below, disrupting the symmetrical mandala; also note the red 'seed' elements in the upwelling material, suggesting a fertilizing potential. One of Haeckel's images, used here for comparison, shows reduced symmetry in the natural world and bears a curious resemblance to Jung's disrupted mandala. In *Memories, Dreams, Reflections*, Jung proceeds at this point to discuss the mandala as giving a picture of the state of the self, but he doesn't return to the problem of the breaking of symmetry – which I suggest ironically relates to the emergence of his own ability to conceive of and relate to the self! In terms of *The Red Book*, the last chapter on the Magician offers this in narrative form: in his struggles with Philemon, Jung seems to be moving from a fascination with the mana personality, especially of the Wise Old Man, toward an experience of the self, but he must go through a rupture of the idealizing projection first (2009: 312ff).

Much later, in the Jung/White correspondence, we see another example of the breaking or reducing of symmetry in a figure of the self as four octahedrons (as Platonic solids) stacked atop one another. In other publications, I have discussed the difference between this version and the version Jung published in *Aion* (see Cambray 2009). In the unpublished figure from the private correspondence, there is a rotation of the top octahedron (as well as other features) that is erased in the highly symmetrized published version in *Aion*. I postulate that these are examples of the ambivalence Jung felt about the lowering or disruption of symmetry in images. The irony stems from knowledge of complex systems (information unavailable to Jung), where self-organization and the emergence of something new (akin to the transcendent function) require the system to undergo a reduction in symmetry as an essential part of the process of transformation. My speculation is that Jung intuitively grasped this but found it emotionally and aesthetically repellant. Those contemporary Jungians interested in complex systems and emergence may wish to study *The Red Book* further for other clues it holds regarding Jung's struggle for a fully emergentist psychology.

The images in *The Red Book* on page 85 reveal the process that had seemed to be deforming the mandala now appears fecund. Where the star had been above the main figure on page 84, now the seeds seem to have coalesced into a self-organizing swarm in the form of a fish, an image Jung amplified at length in *Aion* – a form of the emergent self. A variety of analogous shapes from nature and Haeckel's engravings offer visual biological amplification, as can be found in Haeckel's *Ascidia* (1904/1998: Plate 85), a sea squirt colony; comparison with a modern schematic of a medusa also reveals nearly identical morphology.

The next three successive images from *The Red Book* indicate increasing complexity and elaboration of an individuation process, if viewed as states of the self. This reaches full flower on page 89, which I suggest draws on a number of images from Haeckel, which are placed in juxtaposition to capture the echoes (see 1904/1998: Plates 23, *Bryozoa*; 84, *Diatomea*; 96, *Chaetopoda, Sabella*; see Haeckel's drawing of Calcareous sponges in Breidbach 2006: 177). The mandala series continues with another set of transformations shown on pages 90 through 97, where a cosmic egg, now filled with multilayered geometric forms, is produced (space does not permit an analysis of these images). I end this series with Plate 6, which shows page 125 of *The Red Book*, alongside several sea squirt images from Haeckel (1904/1998: Plate 84).

Haeckel's influence on contemporary art and some possibilities for *The Red Book*

In recent years, there has been a rekindling of interest in *biomimetic* art, perhaps due to new paradigms emerging in the biological sciences. Some of the artists who have been producing this work acknowledge a debt to Haeckel and/or the philosophy of ornamentation associated with his work (as potentially revealing the depth of nature). There are several illustrative examples to which I would like to draw attention. First is the art of Fred Tomaselli, whose work is exhibited by the James Cohan Gallery in New York City (see http://www.jamescohan.com/artists/fred-tomaselli/). In discussing his artwork, Tomaselli has noted 'that Haeckel's mirror-image arrangements propose, in effect, their own meta-organism, a more-than-perfect symmetry which plays upon the "idea of the beautiful as it is coded deep within us"' (Brody 2002). Furthermore, in recent years James Cohan (the owner of the gallery) has become interested in Jung and Jungian ideas – an indicator of a resonance with the influences discussed in this paper reemerging in contemporary culture.

A second working artist who shares these resonances is Philip Taaffe. In his writings, Taaffe clearly admires Haeckel, noting how he brought draftmanship 'to a new level of authority or life or animation . . . The brilliance of the graphic execution is undeniable; you have to be aware of these. You have to look and look,' even though he finds Haeckel's *Art Forms* 'too willful, too aestheticized to use' (Brody 2002). In addition, Taaffe is one of the artists who has engaged in the Rubin dialogues on *The Red Book* – a series of public events in which 'personalities from many different walks of life were paired on stage with a psychoanalyst and invited to respond to and interpret a folio from Jung's *Red Book* as a starting point for a wide-ranging conversation.' Thus the impact of Haeckel's work on Jung continues to have ripples in the modern world.

A third example is of biomimetic architecture in the work of Zaha Hadid. Plate 7 compares her work to a plate by Haeckel on platodes. Referring to this structure by Hadid, which was placed on the cover of the journal *Social Text*, the editors comment:

> The design by Zaha Hadid Architects for the Abu Dhabi Performing Arts Centre – a new cultural institution for the Solomon R. Guggenheim Foundation – was unveiled in January 2007. . . . Hadid describes her multitiered design as 'a sculptural form that emerges from a linear intersection of pedestrian paths within the cultural district . . . a growing organism that sprouts a network of successive branches.'[5].

These are but a sampling.

What will this mean for the reception of *The Red Book?* That, of course, remains to be seen, but I would look to the impact the book will have on American arts and aesthetics as much as on psychology. I hope it challenges us to more fully integrate the aesthetic dimension of imagery into our theory and practice, including archetypal theory with its neurobiological roots. We could draw on new areas of research, such as neuroesthetics, speculations on neuro-art history (as in the writings of John Onians and Semir Zeki), as well as the relationship between various arts and evolutionary models; for example, in 2009, Denis Dutton published *The Art Instinct*, a book exploring these links. In this, perhaps we will be able to more clearly articulate the archetypal base of the feeling function and bring it into a wider discourse with other disciplines. Similarly, we may wish to engage with contemporary views on memory, the relationship among culture, learning, behavior, and evolution; and reevaluate the notion of the phylogeny of the psyche. However, before wrapping up, there is one more entrance and exit I would like to address briefly.

The Red Book and the end of prophecy

As we already know from *Memories, Dreams, Reflections*, Jung had a set of visions starting in October 1913 that made him fear for his sanity. Shamdasani addresses this directly in his introduction to *The Red Book*:

> The following month [October 1913], on a train journey to Schaffhausen, Jung experienced a waking vision of Europe being devastated by a catastrophic flood, which was repeated two weeks later, on the same journey. . . . Commenting on this experience in 1925, he remarked: 'I could be taken as Switzerland fenced in by mountains and the submergence of the world could be the debris of my former relationships.' This led him to the following diagnosis of his condition: 'I thought to myself, "if this means anything, it means that I am hopelessly off."' . . . He recalled that he first thought that the images of the vision indicated a revolution, but as he could not imagine this, he concluded that he was 'menaced with a psychosis.'
>
> (Jung 1963: 200; Jung 2009: 198)

After providing several more of Jung's visions and his reflections, Shamdasani reports on how Jung felt in 1914: 'I had the feeling that I was an over-compensated psychosis, and from this feeling I was not released until August 1st 1914' (Jung 1989: 44; 2009: 201). Shamdasani notes that Jung was released from this horror when the war broke out, and he had to take a ship to get home, as in one of his dreams, so that his experiences could be read as precognitions: 'At this moment, Jung considered that his fantasy had depicted not what would happen to *him*, but to Europe' (202). Extrapolating,

Shamdasani argues, Jung went on to examine other fantasies to see if there were a correspondence between private fantasies and public events. 'This effort makes up much of the subject matter of *Liber Novus*' (202). He proceeds to list twelve separate fantasies that he feels Jung may have regarded as precognitive (202). Here, the entrance is found in the tension between prophecy and madness.

In *Liber Novus*, Jung struggles with his affective responses to Salome, whom we might view as the anima of the prophet:

> Elijah said: 'You should recognize her through her love!' Not only do you venerate the object, but the object also sanctifies you. Salome loved the prophet, and this sanctified her. The prophet loved God, and this sanctified him. But Salome did not love God, and this profaned her. But the prophet did not love Salome, and this profaned him. And thus they were each other's poison and death.
>
> (2009: 248)

Jung wrestles with his feelings about his furtive, paradoxical love of prophecy, feeling on the one hand that it has redeemed him, yet on the other a dawning concern that it threatens him with a confusion of the personal and the archetypal, as in his becoming the leontocephalus, which was one of the forms of Phanes (from the first mandala image). Although I do not have space here to examine Jung's working through of this problem, I would like to turn briefly to some of the results.

In *Liber Secundus*, especially in the Magician chapter, the encounters with Elijah and Salome are picked up again. Elijah 'gives' a sighted Salome to Jung, and he is highly ambivalent: 'It seems to me a rather strange gift [Salome], more burden than joy. I am happy that Salome is thankful to me and loves me. I love her too – somewhat' (2009: 323). Salome tries to offer herself to him; Jung tries to handle her love for him as if an erotic transference, valuing it while remaining distant. She sees through this saying, 'Why only speak? I want to be yours, utterly and completely yours,' which drives Jung to a sharper reply: 'You are like the serpent that coiled around me and pressed out my blood. Your sweet words wind around me and I stand like someone crucified' (323). They continue this awkward banter. Finally Elijah intervenes and supports Jung in his wish for autonomy: 'May each one carry his load. He who wants to burden others with his baggage is their slave.' Salome responds, 'But father, couldn't I help him bear part of his burden.' Elijah replies, 'Then he'd be your slave' (323). With this, Jung seems to find his own ground and speaks at length to both of them about being near yet remaining autonomous.

Taking Salome as the anima state associated with Jung's prophetic ambitions and anxieties, this exchange seems a crucial element in his differentiating himself from the personalistic trappings of becoming the prophet himself. Further, he now can see that the figure of 'Philemon' stands behind his imaginings and that he can differentiate himself from him. As Shamdasani notes: 'He [Jung] realized that there was a prophetic wise old man in him, to whom he was not identical' (2009: 207). Jung extricates himself from a state of possession by this archetype, becoming angry at Philemon and telling him he is the

> most cunning of all fraudsters! You have deceived me. You impregnated my maidenly soul with the terrible worm . . . you played a Christ-fool's comedy with me, you hanged me, carefully and ludicrously, in the tree just like Odin, you let me devise runes to enchant Salome.
>
> (327)

I believe this is the point at which Jung comes to differentiate the archetype of the Wise Old Man from a deeper experience of the self. What then is the exit this leads to?

In the epilogue to *The Red Book* Jung writes:

> My acquaintance with alchemy in 1930 took me away from it. The beginning of the end came in 1928, when Wilhelm sent me the text of the 'Golden flower,' an alchemical treatise. There the contents of this book found their way into actuality and I could no longer continue working on it.
>
> (2009: 360)

In *Memories, Dreams, Reflections,* Jung also identifies a deeply meaningful synchronistic occurrence here – that is, his painting of 'a mandala with a golden castle in the center' having a curiously Chinese feeling about it, just prior to receipt of the manuscript from Richard Wilhelm (1963: 197). He contextualizes this further, offering a dream that presages the events. This is the Liverpool dream (of 1927) in which he makes his way to a place where:

> [t]he various quarters of the city were arranged radially around the square. In the center was a round pool, and in the middle of it a small island. While everything round about was obscured by rain, fog, smoke, and dimly lit darkness, the little island blazed with sunlight. On it stood a single tree, a magnolia, in a shower of reddish blossoms. It was as though the tree stood in the sunlight and were at the same time the source of light. My companions commented on the abominable weather, and obviously did not see the tree. They spoke of another Swiss who was living in Liverpool, and expressed surprise that he should have settled here. I was carried away by the beauty of the flowering tree and the sunlit island, and thought, 'I know very well why he has settled here.' Then I awoke.
>
> (198)

In his comments on this mandalic center, Jung attends to the name of the city, Liverpool, which he takes to mean the pool of life. There is a fascinating echo here to the dreams of his 19-year-old self, with the giant radiolarian in the forest pool, now more fully realized. Shamdasani takes Jung's commentary on *The Secret of the Golden Flower* as a turning point; it was his first public discussion of the significance of the mandala. I agree, but think there is a further point here.

As his confrontation with the unconscious draws to a close, Jung notes the confrontation with the world begins. Shamdasani comments:

> In retrospect he described the *Red Book* as an attempt to formulate things in terms of revelation. He had hoped that this would free him, but found that it didn't. He then realized that he had to return to the human side and to science. He had to draw conclusions from the insights.
>
> (2009: 219)

On the next page Shamdasani does make a link to Jung's essay on synchronicity:

> In 1952, through his collaboration with the Nobel prize-winning physicist Wolfgang Pauli, Jung argued that there existed in principle of acausal orderedness that underlay such 'meaningful coincidences,' which he called synchronicity. . . . This was an attempt to expand scientific understanding to accommodate events such as his visions of 1913 and 1914.
>
> (220)

While accurate, this overlooks the historical timing of Jung's actual, original formulation of the concept of synchronicity. In the first chapter of my book on synchronicity (Cambray 2009), I detail how the term first arose in Jung's dream seminars in 1928 (the same year as he received the *Golden Flower* text); in one of the seminars, other synchronistic clusters of dreams and images were also being discussed. Then, in 1930, Jung for the very first time used the term *synchronicity* at Richard Wilhelm's memorial service. From these facts, I argue that it is precisely Jung's ability to formulate this new idea, to bring forth a genuinely novel, creative thought, one that could be brought into existence for the larger scientific world that is the key discovery/act that moved him beyond prophecy. Synchronicity, as an attempt to conceive and come to terms with events that had been viewed as prophetic but now might be made amenable to scientific reflection, is, for me, the true exit Jung took from *The Red Book* into his confrontation with the world. Jung is attempting a transformation in culture from a theological to a psychological ground.

It then remains for us to unpack this further, which is why elaborating the scientific understanding of synchronicity is so directly and intimately tied to the end of his work on *The Red Book.* Recent work by Jungians, myself included, on linking contemporary forms of holistic science such as complexity, emergence, and field theory can be reconsidered now in light of Jung's deliberate decision to end work on *The Red Book* and embrace a synchronistic vision. For example, in 'Psychology and Literature,' one of the papers he wrote at this time, he articulates two modes of artistic creation: the psychological and the visionary (1930/1966). The end of prophecy, as a personal calling or event in this narrative, is concomitant with the awareness that the conscious mind is not the true author of our visions/dreams/imaginings but that the personal sense of self rests upon the archetypal. Such awareness is probably most readily grasped in contemporary idiom by embracing a view of the self as an emergent phenomenon, which I feel follows the trajectory of Jung's entire opus and is one of the more important meanings we can derive from the ending of *The Red Book.*

Notes

1 For a discussion on the relevance of nineteenth-century theories of organic and ancestral memories to Jung's archetypal theory, see Shamdasani (2003: 182–91). In this section, Shamdasani examines links between Semon, who was a student of Haeckel's and Jung's chief, Eugen Bleuler, as well as his former chief August Forel, for their relevance to Jung's ideas.

2 There are additional political dimensions to Jung's relations with Haeckel's ideas, but these will need to be developed in another essay. Recent publications, especially Robert J. Richards' biography of Haeckel (2008) suggest important reconsiderations about the way Haeckel's views may have been misused by some twentieth-century historians. There is also potential relevance for how Jung is to be seen by historians.

3 See the *American Heritage Stedman's Medical Dictionary* at http://dictionary.reference.com/browse/epigenesis for more information.

4 For clarification, at Chateau d'Oex, Jung was commander of the internment camp for escaped British prisoners of war. As Barbara Hannah notes, 'When prisoners of war escaped and made their way into Switzerland, as a neutral country she accepted them but was bound to intern them so that they could not make their way back to their own country and fight again' (1976: 126).

Also, note that in *Memories, Dreams, Reflections*, Jung misremembers the dates as being in 1918–19 when he drew the mandalas (1963: 195).

5 From the back cover of the journal *Social Text*, 'About the Cover Art,' (Lim Eng-Beng 2009: http://socialtext.dukejournals.org/cgi/issue_pdf/backmatter_pdf/27/4_101.pdf.)

References

Breidbach, Olaf (2006) *Visions of Nature: The Art and Science of Ernst Haeckel*, Munich, London: Prestel.

Brody, David. (2002) 'Ernst Haeckel and the Microbial Baroque,' *Cabinet* 7.

Cambray, Joseph (2009) *Synchronicity: Nature & Psyche in an Interconnected Universe*, College Station, Texas: Texas A & M University Press.

Darwin, Charles (1859) *On the Origin of Species by Means of Natural Selection*, First edition. Available online at http://www.talkorigins.org/faqs/origin.html (accessed May 7, 2013).

Dutton, Denis (2009) *The Art Instinct: Beauty, Pleasure, and Human Evolution*, New York, Berlin, London: Bloomsbury Press.

Ellenberger, Henri F. (1970) *The Discovery of the Unconscious: The History and Evolution of Dynamic Psychiatry*, New York: Basic Books, Inc.

Freud, Sigmund (1905) *Three Essays on the Theory of Sexuality*, in J. Strachey (ed.), *The Standard Edition of the Complete Psychological Works of Sigmund Freud*, Volume VII, London: The Hogarth Press.

—— (1916/1963) *Introductory Lectures on Psychoanalysis*, in J. Strachey (ed.), *The Standard Edition of the Complete Psychological Works of Sigmund Freud*, Volume XV, London: The Hogarth Press.

Freud, Sigmund and Ferenczi, Sándor (1996) *The Correspondence of Sigmund Freud and Sándor Ferenczi, Volume 2, 1914–1919*, eds Ernst Falzeder and Eva Brabant, Cambridge MA and London: Harvard University Press.

Giegerich, Wolfgang (1975) 'Ontogeny = Phylogeny? A Fundamental Critique of Erich Neumann's Analytical Psychology,' *Spring*: 110–29.

Goldberg, Aaron, Allis, C. Davi, and Bernstein, Emily (2007) 'Epigenetics: A Landscape Takes Shape,' *Cell* 128, 4.

Gould, Stephen Jay (1977) *Ontogeny and Phylogeny*, Cambridge, MA and London: Harvard University Press.

Haeckel, Ernst (1904/1998) *Kunstformen der Natur*, Leipzig and Vienna: Bibliographisches Institut [*Art Forms in Nature*, Munich, Berlin, London, New York: Prestel Verlag].

Hannah, Barbara (1976) *Jung: His Life and Work, A Biographical Memoir*, Boston: Shambhala Publications.

Jacobi, Jolande (1959) *Complex, Archetype, Symbol in the Psychology of C. G. Jung*, Princeton: Princeton University Press.

Jung, C. G. (1916/1969) 'On the Psychology of the Unconscious,' in *Two Essays on Analytical Psychology, The Collected Works of C. G. Jung*, vol. 7, Princeton: Princeton University Press.

—— (1919/1960) 'Instinct and the Unconscious' in Herbert Read, Michael Fordham, Gerhard Adler (eds) *The Structure and Dynamics of the Psyche, The Collected Works of C. G. Jung*, vol. 8, Princeton: Princeton University Press.

—— (1928/1954) 'Child Development and Education' in Herbert Read, Michael Fordham, Gerhard Adler (eds) *The Development of Personality, The Collected Works of C. G. Jung*, vol. 17, Princeton: Princeton University Press.

—— (1930/1966) Psychology and Literature, *The Spirit in Man, Art, and Literature, The Collected Works of C. G. Jung*, vol. 15, Princeton: Princeton University Press.

—— (1946/1954) 'The Gifted Child' in Herbert Read, Michael Fordham, Gerhard Adler (eds) *The Development of Personality, The Collected Works of C. G. Jung*, vol. 17, Princeton: Princeton University Press.

—— (1963) *Memories, Dreams, Reflections*, New York: Vintage Books.

—— (1975) *Letters, Vol. 2: 1951–1961*, eds Gerhard Adler and Aniela Jaffe, Princeton: Princeton University Press.

—— (1989) *Analytical Psychology: Notes of the Seminar Given in 1925*, ed. William McGuire, Princeton: Princeton University Press.

—— (2008) *Children's Dreams: Notes from the Seminar Given in 1936–1940*, eds Lorenz Jung and Maria Meyer-Grass, trans. Ernst Falzeder with the collaboration of Tony Woolfson, Princeton and Oxford: Princeton University Press.

—— (2009) *The Red Book: Liber Novus*, ed. Sonu Shamdasani, New York, London: W. Norton & Company.
McGuire, William (ed.) (1974) *The Freud/Jung Letters: The Correspondence between Sigmund Freud and C. G. Jung*, trans., Ralph Manheim and R. F. C. Hull, Princeton: Princeton University Press.
Morton, Marsha (2009) '*From* Monera *to Man*, Ernst Haeckel, *Darwinismus*, and Nineteenth-Century German Art,' in Barbara Larson and Fae Brauer (eds), *The Art of Evolution*, Lebanon, NH: Dartmouth College Press.
Richards, Robert J. (2008) *The Tragic Sense of Life: Ernst Haeckel and the Struggle over Evolutionary Thought*, Chicago, London: University of Chicago Press.
Schacter, Daniel L. (2001) *Forgotten Ideas, Neglected Pioneers: Richard Semon and the Story of Memory*, Philadelphia: Psychology Press.
Shamdasani, Sonu (2003) *Jung and the Making of Modern Psychology: The Dream of a Science*, Cambridge: Cambridge University Press.
Taylor, Mark C. (2001) *The Moment of Complexity: Emerging Network Culture*, Chicago: University of Chicago Press.

4

C. G. JUNG IN EASTERN CULTURE AND *THE RED BOOK*

How *The Red Book* helps make Jung more understandable to the traditions of Asia

Bou-Yong Rhi

For this paper, I was assigned the task of answering the question: how does *The Red Book* help make Jung more understandable to the traditions of Asia? The question looks clear and simple. The answer might not be difficult. If considered carefully, however, answering this question is not such a simple task.

In Korea, *The Red Book* is not yet known well, except among a few Jungians, myself included, who bought it on Amazon.com and who have regularly met for reading and discussion since March 2010. Therefore, I am not able to say anything definitively about the influence of the book on the public's understanding of Jung's thought.

The participants in *The Red Book* reading group have had a positive response to *The Red Book*, as one would expect. The reactions of Jungians and those who sympathize with Jung, however, might differ from those of other people. As Jungians, we are coming from the basis of our understanding of the collective unconscious, and, therefore, we may tolerate Jung's archetypal experiences more than others. Individuals may also react differently to Jungian psychology or *The Red Book* according to their psychological type. Distinguishing specific traditional cultural factors from the total reactions of people toward Jungian psychology or *The Red Book* is not easy.

Based on these considerations, I have decided to approach the task by dealing with the things most familiar to me:(1) Korean traditional religious cultures, (2) myself and my own experiences of Jungian psychology since 1962, (3) the 'acculturation process' of Jungian psychology that I have experienced and observed in the West and in the East, and (4) my experiences in reading *The Red Book*.

Asian tradition and its complexity

Far Eastern countries share four major traditional religious cultures: Buddhism, Taoism, Confucianism, and shamanism. Shamanism is the common cultural base of China, Korea, and Japan. The magico-religious systems of *wu* in China, *mudang* in Korea, and *miko* in Japan are very old and closely connected with central Asian and Siberian shamanism.

The rise and fall of, and the reciprocal assimilation or antagonisms among, these four religious cultures can be seen in each country's history. For example, in Korea (see Plate 8), from the Three Kingdoms and the unified Silla Period (57–931 CE) until the end of the Koryo dynasty (931–1391), Buddhism flourished and became the dominant religious culture. During the Three Kingdoms period, people's lives were strongly influenced by shamanism, and shamanistic culture enjoyed high social status. At that time, both shamanism and Buddhism coexisted easily. By the end of the Koryo dynasty, however, these religions had fallen into decay, and in their place, Confucianism arose. The Chosun dynasty (1392–1897), at its founding, declared Confucianism to be its official political doctrine, and Confucianism remained dominant for over 500 years. When modern Western cultures were allowed to disseminate in Korea, Christianity gradually propagated in spite of occasional persecution. Particularly in Korea, in contrast to the other Asian nations, the success of Christianity has been significant.

In modern times, along with rapid industrialization, people's value systems have been radically changed, particularly regarding the traditional system of social rank and deference. The Confucian virtue of modesty has also been challenged, contributing to the rise of military coups. Positive changes include an increase in women's rights and a greater sense of individuality. When closely examined, however, the Korean people remain deeply influenced by traditional cultural values.

Religious cultural spectrums and personality

As an aid in understanding people, including patients from various cultural backgrounds, in the 1990s, I proposed seeing individuals as consisting of various religious cultural elements. Outwardly, he or she may be a Buddhist or a Christian, but the cross-section of his or her personality may reveal manifold religious complexes (Rhi 1998).

Plate 9 represents a person who, apparently Buddhist, has, at the same time, Confucian complexes and an underlying personality comprised of shamanistic passions. Christians are not only Christians, for they too possess an enormous number of Confucian complexes and, at their core, a shamanistic worldview. In Korea, the Taoist component is rather weak compared with China and Taiwan. Confucianism used to be antagonistic toward shamanism, like Christianity toward paganism, but the shamanistic tradition is deeply embedded in the culture.

All these religious cultures possess common denominators: they all focus on the numinosum and the sense of a transcendent existence. In Buddhism, it is called *Jinyeo, tatagata garba;* in Taoism, *Tao;* in Confucianism, *Cheon*, the heaven, or heaven's decree; and in shamanism, it can be seen in ecstatic union with the gods. Some mystic colorings are found in each to different degrees, the least in Confucianism. All religions aim at the actualization of wholeness through self-realization or self-cultivation in various ways according to their specific traditions. Thus, we can observe in the ideas and practices of Eastern religions, symbolically or practically, the individuation process as described by C. G. Jung.

In spite of a common goal and intention, each religious culture reveals a subtle, sometimes even striking, difference in its approach toward self-cultivation. When generally comparing these four religious traditions to Jung's thought, I would say that the ideas closest to Jungian psychology might be in Mahayana Buddhism, in the idea of *Gui il sim won*, or Returning to One Mind. But Seon (Zen) Buddhism seems to have a unique attitude toward the world of images, in that practitioners try to eliminate images to reach enlightenment, *sam_dhi*, or 'dreamless and imageless serenity.'

Confucianism can be regarded as the least coincident with Jung insofar as Confucius did not deal with issues of irrational chaos, demons, and the problems of death. Confucius also rarely mentioned children and women. The Confucian Tao, or way, is different from the Tao of Lao Zi. In Jungian terms, it may be closer to persona. When Confucian thoughts were adopted as a ruling ideology, popularized, and codified for the people during the Chosun dynasty, they dictated a fixed rigid persona and lost the master's original flexibility. The Confucian appreciation for order, discipline, self-reflection, the esthetic, as well as the harmonious relationship between the living and their ancestors and between men and women are based on the principles of reason. Therefore, the Confucianists largely rejected shamanism as an ecstatic religion. Where Confucian culture prevails in a village, shamanic activities are hardly found, except for the New Year's village festival, when the shaman is allowed to practice his or her art after the Confucian ceremony for worshipping the heavenly ancestors.

Shamanism has served in human history as a vessel, in which the primordial patterns of human behaviors are contained and produced incessantly. Above all, the meaning of suffering is strongly emphasized in the initiation process of Korean shamanism, as seen particularly in the middle and northern districts of Korea. *The Red Book* contains initiatory rites such as torture and dismemberment. Korean shamanism has partially assimilated Buddhistic and Taoistic components, and Buddhism has accepted the shamanistic folk belief of the mountain spirit. Thus, these three religions can coexist in relatively friendly circumstances. In some cases, shamanistic culture even assimilated the Christian church service into the shamanic ecstatic way. On the other hand, shamanistic culture has always played the 'shadow' role to reason-oriented Confucianism.

My encountering the West in Jungian analysis

Fact: A man from the East coming to the West for the first time and undergoing personal analysis by a Westerner is not the simplest thing.

In the early stage of my analysis with Dr. Riklin in 1962 at the C. G. Jung Institute in Zürich, I had the feeling that his interpretations of my dreams presented nothing that I did not already know. Therefore, I began to doubt the role of dream interpretation in the search for the unconscious. I asked him, 'Why do you Westerners divide consciousness and the unconscious?' I soon realized that I was incorrect, due to my lack of understanding German and of enough experience. I probably projected my unconscious dichotomizing and discriminating tendency, *bunbyeol-ji* (*vikalpa-buddhi*), onto the 'Westerner.'

During the course of adjusting to European culture and Jungian psychology, I found myself and discovered that I am an extremely introverted Easterner who possesses a very extraverted Confucian persona, which I had never expected to be the case.

Difficulties in communication were because of not only the *Weltanschauung* or language problem but also the forms of verbal expression. For example, when I was asked questions, my verbal expression of yes or no was not clear enough, whether it concerned my feelings or my opinions. My answer was always in between. I sought to adjust myself to the expectations of others – I seemed to find an answer in harmony with the whole situation, instead of showing my 'I in front of the You.' In expressing good and bad, I was also vague. At times I expressed my feelings in a consciously vague manner because precisely selecting between two opposites was unnatural and against the Eastern way of expression, namely, to 'moderate one's light' (Lao Tzu 1989).

I recall expressing myself in that way in response to the usual German greeting, '*Wie geht es Ihnen*?' (How are you?) I replied, '*Es geht mir so ziemlich.*' (Just so-so.) The Swiss students were astonished and shouted, 'What is wrong with you?' I realized then that in the West I should say 'good,' not answer in the Korean way, 'so-so.' I still observe the same tendencies in other Koreans and in myself. When I read in *The Red Book* about the intense confrontation between Jung's I and You, whatever it may be called, I see the differing attitudes between the West and the East in the encountering of I and You.

Still I resisted the active expression of unconscious images. In my dreams, I frequently found that I was painting, so Dr. Riklin recommended that I actually paint. I was reluctant to do so. I thought, I painted already with satisfaction in my dreams, why should I 'exteriorize it arbitrarily?' Exteriorizing inner things seemed to me to do violence to the inner value of the dream. As I didn't follow his recommendation, he became angry. I finally painted and found more satisfaction than I had expected. I preferred keeping precious things within myself, without knowing at that time that I was perhaps responding to Lao Tzu's *De Jing* where the sage keeps his treasure in his bosom and wears rags like common people (Lao Tzu 1989: ch. 70, *Dao*).

Gradually, I adjusted to European culture. I assimilated fairly well into the Western way of life, and my analysis was carried out much more fruitfully with Dr. M. L. von Franz during the latter half of my studies at the Institute. One day I suddenly sensed that my unconscious really existed and acted like a living creature within myself. So I became a Jungian analyst in 1966.

Jungian analysis in Korean culture

In 1968 when I returned home, I recognized that I had changed. I had become Westernized, more extroverted in the true sense, and more individualized, without any inclination toward social prestige. In analysis with Koreans, I met the same difficulties that my 'Western' analysts probably had with me at the beginning of my studies in Zürich. I recognized some remarkable patterns of behavior among my Korean analysands: frequent dropping out of analysis without any notice; magical expectation toward the analyst; a preference for nonverbal communication; some peculiar concepts of body and mind, inclining to extremely concrete somatic views of psychosomatic phenomena; the use of ready-made interpretations of dreams that hampered adequately understanding their meaning.

These culturally conditioned attitudes of consciousness, however, cannot be considered absolute reasons for a failed analysis. I realized that we needed more time to integrate the contents of consciousness before we plunged into the depths of the unconscious. I recognized the coexistence of two contrasting attitudes toward the inexplicable among the Korean analysands: one, a tendency to mystify the nature of matter, two, a concretistic, materialistic, and discriminating tendency. The former, mystifying point of view represented the conscious attitude; the latter concretistic view represented the unconscious. I thought that the latter might be the shadow side of a people who suppressed a preference for an irrational mode of thinking.

I recognized that the most unfavorable and most pernicious precondition for analysis was not complete unconsciousness but semiconsciousness. At that time, I thought the situation in Korea demanded, first of all, a clear distinction between good and evil, rational and irrational, consciousness and the unconscious as a kind of transitional process before setting out on the way of individuation. It was my impression that rational discriminative functions were largely repressed into the unconscious of the Korean analysands because of the dominating irrational tendencies of their consciousness. In the West, it is quite correct to think of consciousness as rational and the unconscious as irrational, but for most Koreans at that time the situation seemed to be reversed (Rhi 1974a).

Many things have changed in the behavioral patterns of the Korean value system since the 1970s. I still have the same opinion regarding the main issues in analysis, however. Jungian analysis always focuses on the individual, and the tasks of maturation of the individual personality, or individuation, are different depending on the analysand's stage of life, as Jung repeatedly stresses in *The Red Book.*

Since 1968, after my return from Switzerland, Jung's analytical psychology has been actively introduced in Korea. Jung was warmly accepted into the circles of Buddhist scholars and students, Protestant theologians, and in the field of literature. Naturally, psychiatrists were the first consumers, and young psychiatrists were very much interested in Jungian analysis (Rhi 2008).

With the first introduction of Jungian psychology in the late 1960s, I didn't want Jungian psychology to become fashionable and popular. I knew Jung's thoughts could spread rapidly, for they draw on the archetypal dimensions of the psyche. I, therefore, made a reserved presentation of Jungian psychology and enforced strict training conditions. In this, my Japanese colleague Professor Kawai and I differed in the manner of introducing and disseminating Jung's thought. The difference lies perhaps in our personal character traits as pioneers and our professional background as well as in the differences in the cultural traditions of both countries.

The result? I see almost the same outcome: the popularization of Jung and the need to maintain the 'true' Jungian identity. It is a challenging question as to what kind of effect and role *The Red Book* will play in the future of this process.

Dialogues with the souls: Korean parallels

The Red Book contains the dialogue between Jung's ego and his unconscious complexes. I wondered whether Eastern approaches to exploring the unknown realm offered a parallel case. Taoistic meditation might be an example, as Jung in collaboration with Wilhelm has demonstrated, but the most classical example might be shamanism (Rhi 1993).

Dialogue with the soul in shamanism

In the initiation process, Siberian and Central Asian shaman candidates undergo a kind of torture by the initiatory spirit. The candidates are totally dismembered to the skeleton and revived again with new flesh and organs. Noteworthy in this process is that the candidates should withstand the torment and observe exactly how the initiation is carried out. In several passages in *The Red Book*, I saw Jung's ego undergo a similarly intense suffering – his initiation process.

The initiation sickness in Korean shamanism is characterized exclusively by signs of contact with gods in visions, dreams, or voices. Noteworthy is that the divine being usually gives orders or recommendations to the dreamer rather than entering any active conversation with the candidates.

The dialogue with the soul between the living and the dead is carried out in the shamanic session called *neokduri*. A mudang, the female shaman, mediates the unresolved grudges and sorrows of the dead to the survivors, producing a highly emotional and moving encounter between the dead and the living. During *gongsu*, or oracle, gods speak through the mouth of the mudang to the client, and then the client reacts emotionally to the gods. To have contact with a god, the induction of a trance state with the help of music and dance is necessary. Dialogue with the souls of the dead and the oracle tend to be stereotypic in their contents within the setting of shamanic rituals. They touch mainly personal complexes. But the myth sung or recited during shamanic rituals contains abundant archetypal material. Jung's active imagination is different from religious meditation in its spontaneity and freedom from fixed rules and procedures. If, however, it is the great shaman who is truly related with his or her helping spirit, (*momju*, or master of my body), shamanism may have the closest parallel to Jung's journey to the underworld and beyond as he described it in *The Red Book.*

Seon (Zen) Meditation

Jung understood Seon (Zen) meditation as an approach to reaching the answer from the total psyche by concentrating on a nonsensical absurd question, or *Hwadu* (*Gong-an, Koan*). He mentioned that the Western equivalent to Seon Buddhism may be psychotherapy (Jung 1939/1969: par. 900 ff). The meditative approach of Seon is the reverse of imagination (*Einbildung*), for in Seon, the ultimate purpose is the elimination of the image as an outer figure – the false image of the world. Even the image of Buddha should be destroyed in Seon Buddhism. The state of truth is a state of tranquility (*Sam_dhi*) – imageless, dreamless serenity.

Naturally, dreams and any irrational images play a role in eliciting enlightenment in the monk; however, one rarely observes the use of dreams or other unconscious images for self-knowledge in Seon. That the Japanese monk, Myokei, had an interest in dreams and used them for introspection is interesting and unusual (Kawai 1987). In terms of Jung's psychology, we may understand the elimination of images in Seon Buddhism as the elimination of the ego's possessiveness of the outer image, that is, the elimination of the concretization of the symbols into signs that can be only be eliminated through assimilation by an adequate understanding of the symbolic meaning of the images.

The Ten Ox Herding Pictures are famous images through which one can learn the path of the Buddha's nature. As they are also somewhat fixed icons, they demand complementation. For the masters who used the pictures for teaching, the pictures served only as stimulation to provoke a creative insight within their mind. The contents of the master's comments and introductory poems to each picture support this suggestion. Jung's comments in *The Red Book* on his inner experiences might have similar significance.

Choe Su-Wun – a creator of a new religion

Choe Su-Wun was a man of early nineteenth-century Korea. He was the creator of the new Korean religion called *Cheon Do Gyo* (Heaven's Road). His enlightenment is connected with a brief mystical experience. At a time when corruption and injustice prevailed in the socioeconomic and political crisis of the nation, which was surrounded by foreign powers, he was steadily searching for the way of redemption (Rhi 1974b).

He delved into Confucian, Buddhist, and Taoist classics for a long time, but he couldn't find the way. He practiced asceticism alone in a cave. One day he felt chilly and shivered. Falling into a trance state, he heard a voice from the air saying; 'I am the heavenly emperor, don't be afraid.' As Su-Wun begged him for teachings, the voice said:

> I possess a mysterious talisman called fairy medicine, its form is gung gung and also taeguk (tai ji) [primary beginning]. Receive this talisman; heal the illness of the people. Receive the magic spell and teach the people; make them like me. You will also live long and will propagate your virtue over all the world.

With great effort, Su-Wun could finally clearly identify the image of the mysterious talisman. His wife had lost all hope, believing he had become mad, and she attempted suicide several times. Upon the recommendation of the heavenly emperor, Su-Wun drew the image of the talisman on a sheet of white paper, burned it, mixed it with clean water, and drank it. Thereafter, he was transformed into a healthier body and his old worries completely disappeared. Later, the heavenly emperor came to him again and tested his virtue, this time by seducing Su-Wun with the promise of power, money, and sorcery. Su Wun strongly rejected these temptations. The heavenly emperor was satisfied and praised him, saying, 'I will give you the endless law of mysterious transformation. My mind is your mind. You have now received my eternal way. Cultivate yourself, teach people.' In that moment, Su-Wun realized that he'd gained new vitality, and the emperor's words rose from the bottom of his mind. From then on he used them to conduct a dialogue with himself. He wrote a song and sang it. He danced with a wooden sword. I have the feeling I've encountered similar dialogues in *The Red Book.*

The main principle of Cheon Do Gyo is *In-Nae-Cheon* – heaven resides within the mind. The religion played a crucial role in the peasant revolt, *Dong-Hak* (The Teachings of the East), and in independent demonstrations under Japanese forced annexation. But the power of this new religion has decreased and survives only among a very limited number of followers.

On *The Red Book*

I have wandered afar and now I come back to the question initially raised. You might be able to estimate how effective or ineffective *The Red Book* will be to the East Asian public for understanding Jung and his psychology. The reactions of the public to the formative aspect of the book and the degree of understanding of its contents vary according to each reader's grasp of Jung's psychology. Even Jung's sympathizers have varied reactions.

It is actually uncertain whether religious traditions in the East play any role in understanding Jungian psychology. Similarity in the various systems of thought can coexist peacefully without reciprocal understanding or any attempt at understanding each other; at the same time, dissimilarities can elicit a collision. But in this collision is the opportunity for mutual understanding through confrontation. The Buddhist monk, the Confucian scholar, Shaman, master of *Gigong* (a Chinese Taoistic psychophysical exercise), or whoever represents the traditions of the East, along with modern Christians may respond positively or negatively to *The Red Book* and also to Jungian psychology. Only those who direct a critical eye to their own religious tradition, however, and seek new attitudes and viewpoints for becoming a whole person can gain understanding. I am not saying that everybody needs to understand Jungian psychology. If in a certain cultural area, traditions are still preserved and active and are appropriate in making the individual a whole person, why should one reject them? The important thing is to know what we are really doing.

What about a Christian? It might be an interesting experiment if you could examine the responses of a Christian to *The Red Book*, which is naturally connected with Jung's critical attitude to conventional Christianity in the West. Moreover, in *The Red Book*, Jung's ego, through active imagination, makes a more vivid confrontation with the problems of evil. Certain Christians might find this awkward. It upsets their peaceful reverence for God and beautiful dependency on the heavenly master as innocent lamb. Jung was brave, declaring what he thought was lacking in the Christian dogma.

Many factors other than religious or cultural factors may influence understanding Jung and *The Red Book.* Primordial fear or fascination with the archetypal components of the unconscious arise more universally among people worldwide than any other factors. Fear and fascination arise frequently together, but if the fascination is dominant and it accelerates the enthusiasm of the public for analytical psychology, contrary to general expectations, it provides unfavorable conditions for the correct understanding of Jung's thoughts. *The Red Book*, I think, has such an infectious power, for it deals with archetypal images.

I will now discuss my personal experiences of *The Red Book.* Before *The Red Book* was published I knew several of Jung's pictures, including those of Philemon and the *Septem Sermones ad Mortuos* from the book edited by Aniela

Jaffé. I didn't clearly understand the motivation for and the meaning of the sermon until I read it in the context of *The Red Book*.

In the mid-1960s I saw the old winged man on the white wall of a small bedroom in Jung's tower at Bollingen. It was so strange to me. I thought, how do I come to understand this man who sleeps under such a strange figure? At that time, I was not fully accustomed to the Jungian approach and was still wandering around in the field of rational philosophical approaches. Today, I would understand someone who reacted to *The Red Book* in the same way, and I would say to him or her, 'Learn the symbols, and experience them. You will then come to understand him.'

The world of images in European cultures was, for the newcomer from Asia like me, strange and shocking unless the images were familiar through previous learning. Images of lions, bears, and serpents are foreign to Asians. Naked human figures, battle scenes, exhibitions of musculature, wrestling scenes, sucking blood, and eating flesh can lead to feelings of disgust and accusations of barbarianism among people of Confucian and Taoistic backgrounds in whom the noble tradition of esthetic tastes have been fostered. Traditional Eastern paintings are aimed principally at expressions of nobility and enlightenment and, as such, exclude ugliness and cruelty. An Eastern painting always has empty space.

Certainly artists have drawn tigers to represent a mountain deity, but most prefer small animals such as monkeys, dogs, cocks, birds, deer, fish, crabs, and cicadas. I see in these the differences between nomadic and agrarian cultures. In *The Red Book*, we can observe the Siberian nomadic tribe's inheritance, and it certainly is connected with Christianity.

I had to read *The Red Book* initially and primarily to fulfill my responsibility as a speaker for the conference from which this book was developed. I read it twice, at first very quickly, a second time in more detail, sometimes comparing the translation with the original German text and making notes. It was a valuable experience for me. I was happy to have the opportunity to read the book. Many things are still obscure, and because the book deals with an enormous range of issues, I do not yet have a full orientation to the book. I have to read it again, this time very slowly. It seems almost a blasphemy to read it quickly, over a few months, and then say something about it, after Jung worked on it for 16 years. Reading it, I felt honored, as if I had been allowed a glimpse of the secret workshop of the great master where masterpieces are almost completed.

The editor of the book, Sonu Shamdasani, kindly and meticulously introduces us to the historical and cultural connections of Jung's 'experimentation' with his soul. This introduction was very instructive. By reading Jung's own words, I soon confirmed that *The Red Book* and Jung's active imaginations were not a psychological experiment like the word association test. He was forced to express these inner images and had to confront them, driven by the irresistible creative forces of his unconscious. It was his destiny, and he followed it.

What Jung wrote in *The Red Book* was the testimony of his initiation process – a process that was not chosen by his experiment-planning ego, but by his innermost Self. Like mystics, he had to undergo the battles with the demonic powers to reach finally the ultimate insight into himself and the world.

The Red Book closely resembles a great epic or a great drama. It is so interesting and impressive. But it is more than that, because we see here enormous pain and torment, the real sufferings of C. G. Jung as a middle-aged man in crisis. He seeks the solution in the midst of conflicts between two opposites. With incessant inquiries into the truth, and through his struggles with the opposing forces, he achieves many insightful discoveries. These are later molded into Jung's theories of analytical psychology in an elaborated form. I was surprised to recognize how his notion of psychic opposites, their union, and the nature of the Self resemble Lao Tzu's *Dao De Jing*. But his major concern was Christianity. He was a Taoistic Christian, which means a man beyond the East and the West.

The destiny, or 'Heaven's Decree' in Confucian terms, that C. G. Jung took on himself was, however, the completion of the Christian dogma. The destiny was already manifested in Jung's childhood when he dreamed of a phallus in the underworld temple, and in his youth, when he saw a vision of God's excrement crushing the beautiful roof of the Münster cathedral in Basel (Jung and Jaffé 1963). I saw, with strong empathy in his search for the nature of God and man's soul depicted in *The Red Book*, his, or his ego's, intense torment, his solicitude, self-criticism, uncertainty, confusion, despair, suspicion, rage, disgust, revolt, and his persistent doubt, as he experienced in his childhood and in his youth.

The words spoken in his imagination are not always gentle, and sometimes very crude. Among them we frequently find the words: 'You lie!' The 'I' in his active imagination may not be identical to C. G. Jung in reality. In *The Red Book*, I was also struck by how plainly he depicted the shadow side of the mind. Disgust, foolishness, mockery, hate, doubt, lying, and so on, are freely expressed. He never tries to beautify the darkness of the psychic world. In this sense, he was absolutely honest with himself.

I noticed in *The Red Book* that no one-sided admiration or respect for authority figures is found. Philemon, for example, who once appeared as a wise old man with glorious authoritative features, was later criticized, and the righteousness of his thought was doubted by the 'I' of Jung. This is remarkable for a person from the East, where reverence toward authority is still partly alive. We have the tradition of *On-Go-I-Ji-Sin* – 'Carry the knowledge gained into new field.' Or 'Take a leaf out of a wise man's book.' This means that we don't destroy the classical thoughts in order to develop new ideas, but we reach new ideas through more intense learning of the classics. Jung mentioned the absence of reverence to authority in the West as one of the differences between East and West (Jung 1939/1969: par. 902).

Jung was worried about being seen as a mad man, and his anima seduced him to be an artist. His worries were warranted. He defended himself in his imagination by letting his ego be admitted to a mental hospital. Jung returned after a long journey into the deep water, however, bringing up from the bottom of the sea a precious piece of the earth – and thus created the world – as told in the Siberian creation myth.

Finally I would like to mention Jung's artistic talent. No doubt, he was a gifted and skillful painter. The atmosphere in his paintings: humidity, light, shadows, air – all the perceptions of the object are sensitively depicted, as if he were a sensation type. In his editing *The Red Book* with its classical German characters and pictographic decorations, I also see characteristics of the Swiss exactitude and accuracy. Naturally, Jung used his artistic skill not for the purpose of artistic creation, but for the expression of the inner image. His pictures are, as Shamdasani has mentioned, like an icon or divine mosaic, and they are designed as if the images are fixed into regular patterns. And the most impressive features are the expressions of inner light. There are many stones, crystals, hard and firm, things, or geometric figures beaming the light from their depths!

He depicted meticulously the figures, the background, and the frames of the pictures with regular patterns, as if he intended to fixate the enormous forces from archetypal images (Jung 1907/1960) or to give pictures of abstract metaphysical implications. The regular patterns reminded me of ancient Chinese patterns of *Docheol* (*Tao-tieh*) on a bronze vessel from the Shang Period (1400–1027 BCE) – the secret of the patterns are not yet elucidated (Brinker 1975).

Figure 4.1 The patterns of the *Tao Tieh* (*Do-Cheol*) on an ancient Chinese bronze vessel.

From *The Red Book* I learned many things. It describes the mind freely without much attempt at strict theoretical formulation; it includes many interesting explanations, simple, direct, and emotionally charged words about life, the nature of the soul, and individuation. We see the strong passion of Jung in his thirties and the reflective comments of Jung in his forties. I am convinced that *The Red Book* shall contribute to understanding Jung in more depth, if one is adequately guided by the Jungian analyst who knows Jung's suffering and its meaning described in the book. For this purpose, studying *The Red Book* among Jungians will be beneficial.

Jung repeatedly emphasizes in his comments in *The Red Book:* 'Be yourself. Don't imitate me!' We read the book not to imitate him, but for *On-Go-I-Ji-Sin* – to discover anew the hidden and neglected meaning of the old experiences by thoroughly studying the thoughts and experiences of C. G. Jung.

References

Brinker, H. (1975) *Bronzen Aus Dem Alten Chia*, Zurich: Museum Rietburg.

Jung, C. G. (1907/1960) 'The Psychology of Dementia Praecox,' in W. McGuire (ed.) *The Psychogenesis of Mental Disease, The Collected Works of C. G. Jung*, vol. 3, Princeton: Princeton University Press.

—— (1939/1969) 'Forward to Suzuki's *Introduction to Zen Buddhism*,'in H. Read, M. Fordham, G. Adler, and W. McGuire (eds) *Psychology and Religion: West and East, The Collected Works of C. G. Jung*, vol. 11, Princeton: Princeton University Press.

—— (2009a) *The Red Book: Liber Novus*, ed. Sonu Shamdasani, trans. Mark Kyburz, John Peck, and Sonu Shamdasani, New York: W. W. Norton and Co.

Jung, C. G. and Jaffé, A. (1963) *Memories, Dreams, Reflections*, New York: Random House.

vai, H. (1987) *Myoé Lives in a Dream (Japanese)*, Kyoto: Kyoto-Sho-Hakusha.

zu (1989) *Tao Te Ching: The Book of Meaning and Life*, London: Penguin Books.

. Y. (1974a.) 'Analysis in Korea with Special Reference to the Question of Success Failure in Analysis,' in G. Adler, (ed.) *Success and Failure in Analysis*, New York: Putnam's Sons.

4b) 'The Mystic Experiences of Choe Su-Wun from a Jungian Viewpoint' *Hnguk Sasang* 11: 5–30.

'The Phenomenology of Korean Shamanism,' in G. Floistad (ed.) *Asian* Dordrect: Kluwer Academic Publishers.

ychiatric Care of Patients with a Shamanistic Cultural Background' *shin Geongang Yeongu* 17: 14–24.

rs of the Korean Society for Analytical Psychology, Past and Future,' *rean Society for Analytical Psychology 1978–2008*, Seoul: The Korean al Psychology.

Ernst Haeckel, *Kunstformen der Natur* (1904), Plate 85, *Ascidiae*

Contemporary electron micrographs of radiolarians

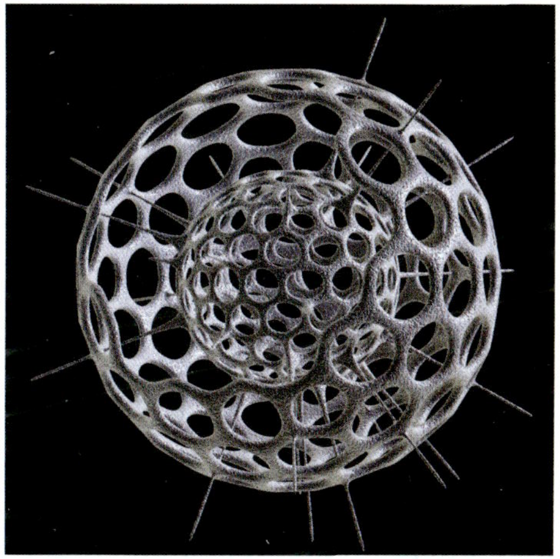

PLATE 1

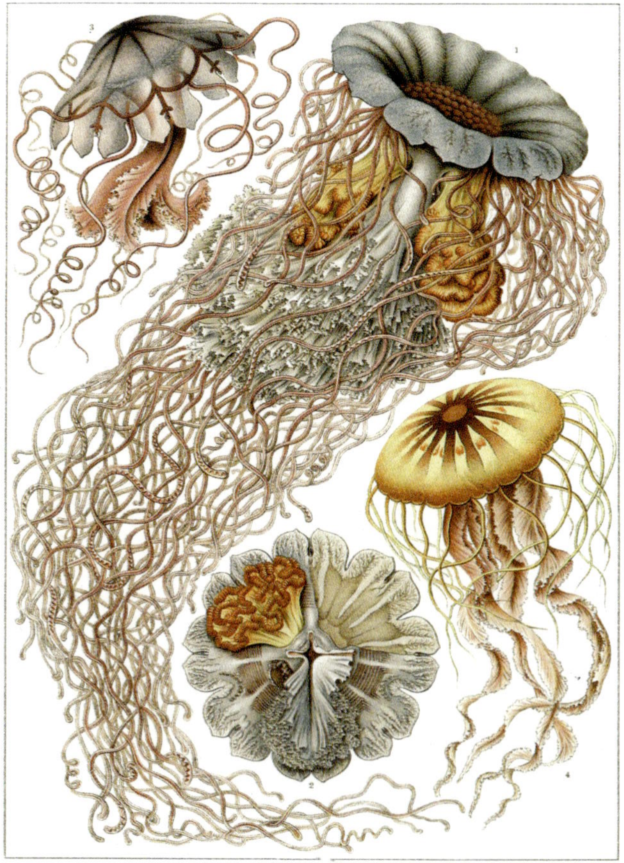

Ernst Haeckel, *Kunstformen der Natur* (1904), Plate 8, *Discomedusae* (central one is *Desmonema Annasethe*)

Contemporary photograph of jellyfish

PLATE 2

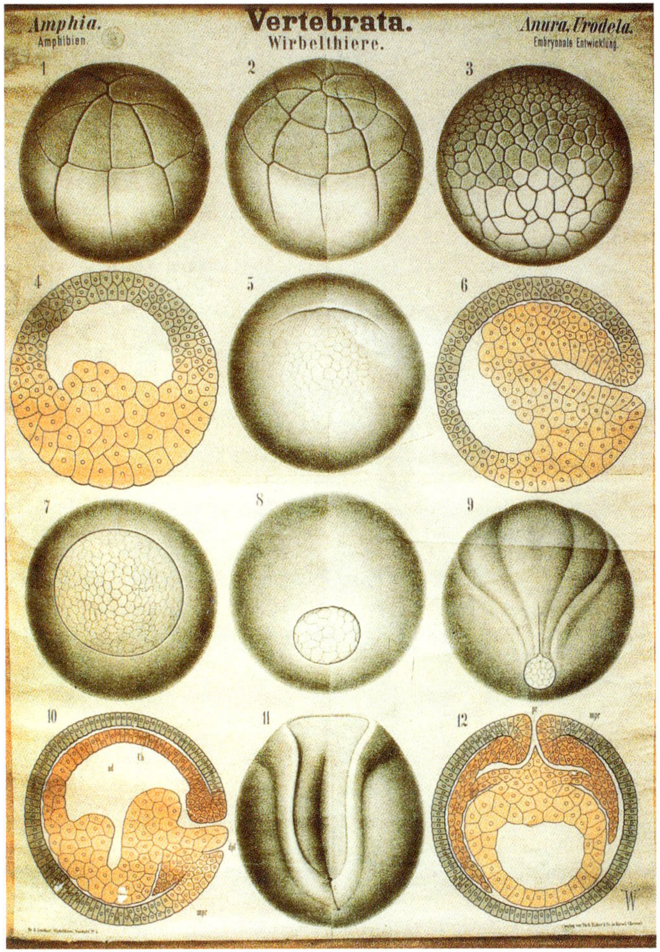

Above: C. G. Jung, *Liber Novus*, from *Liber Secundus*, p. 32. (Used by permission of W. W. Norton & Company, Inc.)

Left: Dr. R. Luckart, Embryonic Development Teaching Chart (1895/96)

PLATE 3

Above: C. G. Jung, *Liber Novus*, from *Liber Secundus*, p. 80. Phanes; metabolism in the individual, original sketch, 2 August 1917. (Used by permission of W. W. Norton & Company, Inc.)

Left: Ernst Haeckel, *Kunstformen der Natur* (1904), Plate 28, *Discomedusae*

PLATE 4

C. G. Jung, *Liber Novus*, from *Liber Secundus*, p. 83. (Used by permission of W.W. Norton & Company, Inc.)

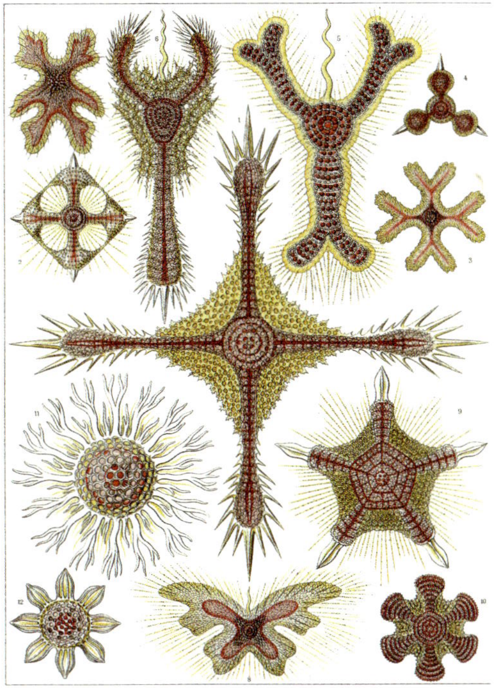

Center: Ernst Haeckel, *Kunstformen der Natur* (1904), Plate 33, *Discoidea*

Right: C. G. Jung, *Liber Novus*, from *Liber Secundus*, p. 84. Broken Symmetry Mandala, original sketch, 6 August 1917. (Used by permission of W.W. Norton & Company, Inc.)

PLATE 5

Ernst Haeckel, *Kunstformen der Natur* (1904), Plate 85, *Ascidiae*

C. G. Jung, *Liber Novus*, from *Liber Secundus*, p. 125. (Used by permission of W. W. Norton & Company, Inc.)

PLATE 6

Above: Zaha Hadid, conceptualization of the Abu Dhabi Performing Arts Center

Left: Ernst Haeckel, *Kunstformen der Natur* (1904), Plate 75, *Platodes*

PLATE 7

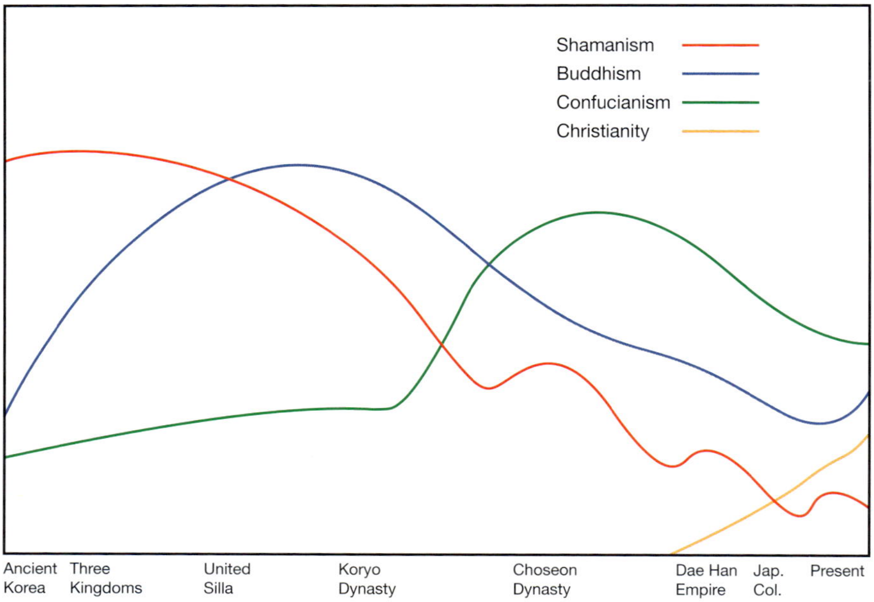

Bou-Yong Rhi, MD, historical rise and fall of religious cultures in Korea

PLATE 8

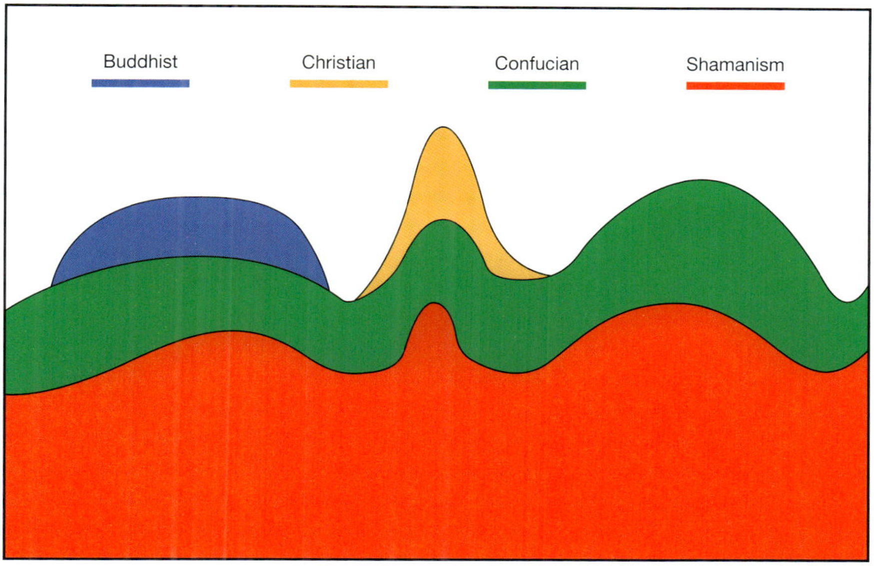

Bou-Yong Rhi, MD, religious/cultural spectrum for individuals (Korea)

PLATE 9

Above: Hilma af Klint, *Ages of Man: Middle-Age, No. 7* from the series *Ten Large Paintings*, 1907, tempera on paper and canvas. (Used by permission of the Hilma af Klint Foundation)

Right: C. G. Jung, *The Red Book*, from Appendix A, p. 361. Mandala sketch, 4 August 1917. (Used by permission of W. W. Norton & Company, Inc.)

PLATE 10

C. G. Jung, *Liber Novus*, from *Liber Primus*, fol. i. (Used by permission of W. W. Norton & Company, Inc.)

PLATE 11

C. G. Jung, *Liber Novus*, from *Liber Secundus*, p. 1. (Used by permission of W. W. Norton & Company, Inc.)

PLATE 12

C. G. Jung, *Liber Novus*, from *Liber Secundus*, p. 11. (Used by permission of W. W. Norton & Company, Inc.)

PLATE 13

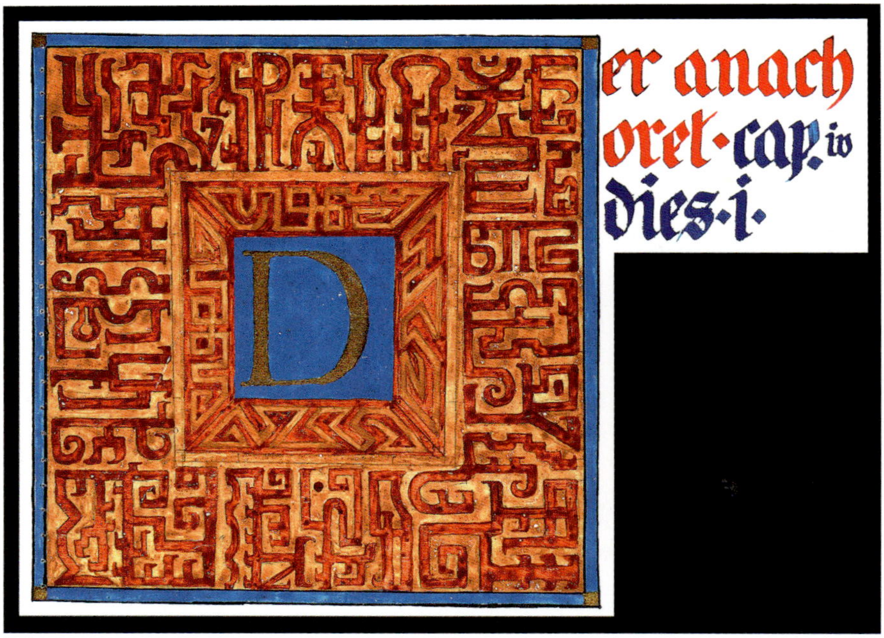

C. G. Jung, *Liber Novus*, from *Liber Secundus*, p. 15. (Used by permission of W. W. Norton & Company, Inc.)

PLATE 14

C. G. Jung, *Liber Novus*, from *Liber Secundus*, p. 22. (Used by permission of W. W. Norton & Company, Inc.)

PLATE 15

C. G. Jung, *Liber Novus*, from *Liber Secundus*, p. 29. (Used by permission of W. W. Norton & Company, Inc.)

PLATE 16

C. G. Jung, *Liber Novus*, from *Liber Secundus*, p. 32. (Used by permission of W. W. Norton & Company, Inc.)

PLATE 17

C. G. Jung, *Liber Novus*, from *Liber Secundus*, p. 36. (Used by permission of W. W. Norton & Company, Inc.)

PLATE 18

C. G. Jung, *Liber Novus*, from *Liber Secundus*, p. 45. (Used by permission of W. W. Norton & Company, Inc.)

PLATE 19

C. G. Jung, *Liber Novus*, from *Liber Secundus*, p. 55. (Used by permission of W. W. Norton & Company, Inc.)

PLATE 20

C. G. Jung, *Liber Novus*, from *Liber Secundus*, p. 64. (Used by permission of W. W. Norton & Company, Inc.)

PLATE 21

C. G. Jung, *Liber Novus*, from *Liber Secundus*, p. 71. (Used by permission of W. W. Norton & Company, Inc.)

PLATE 22

C. G. Jung, *Liber Novus*, from *Liber Secundus*, p. 72. (Used by permission of W. W. Norton & Company, Inc.)

PLATE 23

C. G. Jung, *Liber Novus*, from *Liber Secundus*, p. 97. (Used by permission of W. W. Norton & Company, Inc.)

PLATE 24

C. G. Jung, *Liber Novus*, from *Liber Secundus*, p. 115. (Used by permission of W. W. Norton & Company, Inc.)

PLATE 25

C. G. Jung, *Liber Novus*, from *Liber Secundus*, p. 119. (Used by permission of W. W. Norton & Company, Inc.)

PLATE 26

C. G. Jung, *Liber Novus*, from *Liber Secundus*, p. 125. (Used by permission of W. W. Norton & Company, Inc.)

PLATE 27

154

the bhagavadgita says: whenever there is a decline of the law and an increase of iniquity, then i put forth myself. for the rescue of the pious and for the destruction of the evildoers, for the establishment of the law i am born in every age.

ΠΡΟΦΗΤΩΝ ΠΑΤΗΡ ΠΟΛΥΦΙΛΟΣ ΦΙΛΗΜΩΝ

Ich gehe meine straße weiter. ein feingeschliffen, in zehn feuern gehärtet stahl, im gewande geborg, ist mein begleit. ein panzerhemd liegt mir um die brust, heiml. unt. d. mantel getrag. üb. nacht gewañ i die schlang lieb, i habe ihr rätsel errath. i setze mi z' ihn auf die heiß steine am wege. i weiß sie listig v grausam z' fang, jene kalt teufel, die d. ahnungslos in die ferse stech. i bin ihr freund geword v blase ihn eine mildtönende flöte. meine höhle ab. schmücke i mit ihr schillernd häut. wie i so mein weg dahinschritt, da kam i z' ein röthlich fels, darauf lag eine große buntschillernde schlange. da i nun beim groß ΦΙΛΗΜΩΝ die magie gelernt hatte, so holte i meine flöte hervor v blies ihr ein süß zauberlied vor, das sie glaub machte, sie sei meine seele. als sie genügend bezaubert war,

C. G. Jung, *Liber Novus*, from *Liber Secundus*, p. 154. (Used by permission of W. W. Norton & Company, Inc.)

PLATE 28

C. G. Jung, *Liber Novus*, from *Liber Secundus*, p. 155. (Used by permission of W. W. Norton & Company, Inc.)

PLATE 29

C. G. Jung, *Liber Novus*, from *Liber Secundus*, p. 159. (Used by permission of W. W. Norton & Company, Inc.)

PLATE 30

Jung, in his everyday 'I,' was afraid that his work would be taken as primarily aesthetic, rather than being seen as the extraordinarily far-reaching project that it was – an attempt to bring into being a new understanding and an actual possibility for the lived human life – a life that could be lived on the basis of the truth of self-knowledge, by withdrawing the projections of the unwanted parts of oneself and accepting them as part of the whole psyche. Facing this truth, a person could then, Jung hoped, relate to his or her community, including the community of the dead, to family, and to the spiritual mystery most often called 'God,' without manipulating or using them, often unconsciously, in an attempt to escape from the fear, the shadow, and the consequent suffering that was so painful to bear.

To accomplish this, the individual could relate to 'The Spirit of the Depths' – the living reality of the unconscious – and could thus help to counteract what Jung called 'The Spirit of the Times,' the entire sociocultural structure so often called 'reality,' by which so many people defined themselves and which also encouraged escape from self-knowledge through compliance with its currently accepted ideals. These ideals, stemming from the contemporary material accomplishments of scientific rationality, with its increasing control of nature and its pragmatic understanding of human nature, spoke their own hyper-rational language of 'use and value.' Jung's intention was to utilize his own techniques – of dream work and active imagination – as well as his personal gift of being able to induce waking vision, to find a way into the walled-off and unconscious aspects of human capability. In this way, he hoped to get at their truth, and through the healing induced by these capabilities, he could produce proof of their viability. This experimental proof could then, in turn, make this method acceptable to the current scientific worldview.

No wonder Jung didn't want his work to be seen, as he said, as 'merely aesthetic,' although surely beauty can produce a kind of fulfillment, not just the unrealistic yearning that Jung accused it of and that he was afraid would militate against the truth-telling that was his project in *The Red Book.*

Before moving into the paintings themselves, I want to make some observations about the 'Spirit of the Times,' as it relates especially to art in Jung's lifetime. In popular journalistic articles, *The Red Book* has been referred to many times as 'medieval' in tone. Its careful calligraphy and its decorated capital letters, technically referred to as *historiated capitals*, are indeed medieval in their inspiration. The same medieval inspiration is also clearly present in *Liber Primus* (*Book One*) in the separate pictures themselves.

There are at least two reasons for the book's medieval quality. First, at the end of *Liber Secundus* (*Book Two*), Jung says, 'I must catch up with a piece of the Middle Ages – within myself. We have only finished the Middle Ages of – others. I must begin early, in the period when the hermits died out' (2009: 330). Later, in 1930, he notes that this regression to the medieval was needed when there was 'an insurmountable obstacle' in one's journey (330, note 354). Second, Jung intuitively felt that the material in his earlier diaries, called the

Black Books because of the color of their covers, should be decorated in as 'costly,' rich, and beautiful a manner as possible. This was a way for him, as it was in the Middle Ages, to honor something spiritually valuable, a holy relic, a chalice used in the mass of a particular holy day, and especially the rare books of the time.

These medieval elements also belong, at least in part, to the great and continuing interest in the medieval in the art and literary movements of that time. Since *The Red Book* appears at first glance so characteristic of the medieval, it is perhaps difficult to recognize it as what it actually is – a great modernist[1] document. I will speak only briefly about this, but it is an important aspect of the book's written text as well as of its pictorial elements. For artists working at the time that *The Red Book* was created, the goals of painting as well as the techniques utilized had changed dramatically during the years before and after the turn of the nineteenth century. First to deliberately and fundamentally change the mode and subject of painting 'reality' were the Impressionists and Post-Impressionists; then came the Fauves in their infamous Parisian exhibition of 1905; and in 1913, the Armory exhibition in the United States, attended by Jung (Sherry 2011), challenged any of the still-remaining Post-Renaissance methods and purposes. Part of modernism was a return to other times and modes of art. Preindustrial, archaic, and foreign subjects and techniques were explored. Boundaries between art and decoration, art and objects of utility, high art and low art, were broken down; and unconscious, fantasy, and supernatural sources were examined for their own sake. Jung utilized all of these modalities later in the art of *Liber Secundus*, the second part of *The Red Book.* Traditional forms of Western culture had broken under the weight of industrialized, scientized, and technologized successes and the resultant struggle to find a viable human life and meaning for that life brought forth a multitude of art movements to deal with the multitude of perceived problems.

As the early Middle Ages were the last time that a more or less unified life, with its center of religious faith, had existed in the West, artists naturally turned in that direction for inspiration. Their desire was for something to replace the dismembered human community and the anxious and fragmented human personality. Think of William Morris (1834–96), whose arts and crafts movement was based on a medievally inspired conviction that handcrafting even the most ordinary implements of daily life 'by the people . . . was a happiness to the maker and [to] the user' (Morris 1882: 64).

Jung's project, then, was to find, within himself, the meaning of his own individual life and the creativity, of whatever sort, to bring this meaning into the everyday world. Since the majority of the paintings in *Liber Secundus* were added a few years after the volcano of his visions of 1913–14, they were painted in a time when 'modernist' art was in the ascendant: it would take another paper even to begin to explore thoroughly all the aspects in which Jung's 'modernism' is revealed. I mention only two anecdotal instances to underline this point.

For the first, I want to call attention to the work and methods of an obscure Swedish artist, Hilma af Klint (1862–1944). She worked alone and had no knowledge of the origins of abstract art. 'She had a very specific creative technique, working through a dialogue between the conscious and the unconscious,' and 'was not able to discuss how and why she came to the persons or forces she referred to as her leaders, gurus, or guides' (Fante 1986: 156). Plate 10 (left) shows one of her images from 1907. Here is someone of whom Jung could have had no personal knowledge, nor she of him. Yet in *The Red Book* (see Plate 10 right) is one of the very first of the mandala images, which Jung sketched by hand in 1917 (2009: 361, lower-left image).

A second modernist anecdote concerns Gustav Klimt, the famous modernist and Secessionist painter, who visited Ravenna in 1905 and a few years later began to incorporate mosaic-like elements into his painting. Jung visited Ravenna in 1914, after which mosaic-like elements appear in several of his paintings for *The Red Book*. Both men would have been attracted to the texture, aliveness, and brilliance of an essentially flat, two-dimensional surface, so different from the concern with realistic perspective of the Post-Renaissance traditions, the flatness of surface echoing one of the main concerns and hallmarks of the modernists: the reality of multiple viewpoints and a concern for the reality of materials.

As I begin to talk about the paintings in *The Red Book*, let us remember that the book is constructed as a series of connected or picaresque episodes, rather than as a completely linear narrative. These episodes, in the experiences that occur to Jung, also constitute a number of circumambulations, as Jung gets closer and closer to his own center and, most importantly, closer to letting go of the idea of his personal center as the solar light. Again, his struggle is enormous and often painfully humiliating. The work of the art in *The Red Book* is also the work on, and of, Jung himself.

The image shown in Plate 11 is the first in *The Red Book* (2009: *Liber Primus* 1; hereafter *LP*). Like the other images in this chapter, it immediately arouses a feeling of a childlike, but not childish, and almost fairy-tale world. The scene in which the capital *D* stands is an apparently idyllic medieval village, painted with only minimal perspective, from the lowest plants and somewhat scary animal life at the bottom of the sea, to the golden sun in the ecliptic of the Zodiac precisely in place. The only clues to actual time are disparate, as they might be in the imagination of a child or in the unconscious. A ship from the European Renaissance Age of Discovery floats in the harbor, but the four-rayed golden sun stands between Pisces and Aquarius, the contemporary astrological moment that Jung considered so important. Two planets are identifiable: Saturn with its rings and Jupiter with three of its moons (the fourth that Galileo saw and the other four discovered since the Renaissance are not included). The moon is waning, and a comet, perhaps a portent of change or disaster, hurtles downward. There is no cross on the church. But far away to the right, along the border of *Der Weg des Kommenden*

('The Way of What is to Come'), things are more aggressive, although the images are so tiny and distant. A formation of men with pikes or spears moves toward a nineteenth-century cannon, which fires back. On the far right, in the middle image, all is peaceful, even the sailboat. However, on the bottom margin, a huge crocodile, or something equally dangerous, begins to climb out onto land. In the center is a feminine vase with a masculine arrow, but they are pictorially unrelated to one another.

Perhaps most portentous is the crowned snake, full of the energy of the earthly fire contained in the vase from which it emerges, but showing us its ambivalence in its dualistic white belly and black skin. The process of change has begun. The fire at the core of the earth, depicted marginally at the bottom of the picture, has begun to move.

I have dwelt at length on this charming painting not only because it seems to present the emotional as well as the literal starting point of Jung's work on himself, but also because it exemplifies the fact that is almost always true of the paintings in *The Red Book*: they are both emotionally arresting and mysterious and constructed so that almost every detail can be read symbolically as well; Jung's own integrative process begins in the very act of painting these pictures. French literary symbolism had had a tremendous effect on all the arts by the time of the modernists, and symbolism on the cultural level held a deep fascination for Jung, even as he cautioned, starting with his 1916 paper on active imagination 'The Transcendent Function' (Jung 1960: 67–91) that on the personal level, and from the point of view of therapeutic technique, the only true symbol was the one that the individual brought forth for him- or herself.

It is a loss that I cannot pause on all the paintings in *Liber Primus*, partly to show the extraordinary connections of style and symbol throughout this book, partly to reveal more clearly the beginnings of Jung's journey, and partly to underscore the childlikeness of the painting. The return to the medieval signals a return to a re-opening of the energies of both the personal and the archetypal unconscious for Jung.

Liber Secundus carries the overall title of '*Die Bilder des Irrenden*' ('The Images of the Erring'). *Bilder* in German can refer either to image or, rhetorically, to metaphor, as image in language. Jung utilizes both in his attempt – the conscious attempt of all modernist writing and painting – to find a language that can speak immediately, can communicate without mediation to the emotional and spiritual, the shadowed, unmoral, and instinctual unconscious of the reader or viewer. As Hugo von Hoffmansthal, the Austrian writer of the period, stated, 'there was more, something more divine, more bestial, and it was the Present, the fullest, most sublime Present' (2005: 124). Also note that in German *Irre*, as an adjective, can also carry the connotation of 'insane,' which was Jung's own most powerful fear for himself as he underwent these experiences, as a wanderer, a knight errant on a quest for the meaning of himself.

In the first image of *Liber Secundus* (p. 1) we see sedimentary layers of rock beneath the water, the same water that formed such a disproportionate portion of the first image of *Liber Primus*, already described. Shamdasani has noted that Jung saw the art of schizophrenics as almost always fissured down the center (2009: 259). Here, in Plate 12, the fissuring (unlike the serpent in the previous historiated capital) cannot be contained within the confines of the letter *D*, but it has not yet, as shifting sedimentary layers would, distorted the surface. The 'Spirit of the Depths' is threatening but not yet disturbing the 'Spirit of the Times.'

The black of the letter *D* creates an ambiguity of space, which can be read either as a presence or as an absence. Instead of the single, crowned, and rising snake that was the transforming element at the beginning of *Liber Primus*, here are the two Kundalini snakes, painted in their typical red and blue, distorted into closed claws at top and bottom, rather than being depicted as creating a new energy, as they would in Tantric practice. Moreover, their joining at the top is held in check and also does not break the water's surface.

A single eye stares out from the center. Is this the single eye of God, as it has been represented in Western iconography? Is it the eye of Horus, lost in his battle with evil in Egyptian mythology? Is it the staring eye of paranoia, in the ultimate projection of what it refuses to see inside and is obsessed with seeing outside? Or is it, with its solar disk as the pupil and its golden surround, the possibility of the individuated sun, locked in its underworld aspect and not yet able to move in the diurnal rhythm of night and day?

In terms of art theory, it could be the single viewpoint of the human observer, unified in Renaissance art by the observer's 'correct' and 'realistic' perspectival placement in front of a carefully constructed painting (Hockney 2001). The unification of this observer within a world ordered by that observer's very act of seeing is, indeed, what broke apart in modernism: the resulting chaos of that broken humanness is what Jung is trying to find his way through and out of by way of this enormous project of accepting every aspect of his own human psyche, creating a new unification and ordering of the individual. Now it is possible to see both the tremendous effort and the tremendous suffering of the seismic shift recorded (but not as a re-presentation) in this painting.

This I think is an answer to Shamdasani's question in his introduction to *The Red Book*, as to why Jung shifted in his painting from a representational style to an abstract and symbolic one. The entire task of *The Red Book* is to find a way, in word-image and painting-image, to speak directly from the 'Spirit of the Depths' and not in the logical scientific mode of the 'Spirit of the Times,' which had separated human beings from one half of their reality, creating a rational and disembodied world that could only re-present and not be in its own life.

From here I will continue with the extraordinary images of *Liber Secundus*, remembering that the third section of *The Red Book*, entitled *Scrutinies*, has no paintings. Choices have had to be made due to constraints on the length of the essay, but I will try to indicate some of the most important and interesting aspects of these paintings. Chapter III, 'One of the Lowly,' also begins with the initial capital (Plate 13) with its shattered background and its hints both of disordered mosaic tesserae and a kind of scattering of seeds, a theme that runs through *The Red Book* (2009: *LS* 11). The certainty of death in the body is Jung's lesson here: 'I saw outer death was better than inner death' (2009: 267). But observe also, even in the scattering chaos of the image, the cone shape arising from the bottom of the image and the still only potentially redeemed red sun of the lower world.

In Chapter IV, 'The Anchorite,' the first capital (Plate 14) uses an almost classical perspective in its unity, with the opening often described in Renaissance treatises as a 'window,' with a deep blue background in the opening that increases the sense of depth (2009: *LS* 15). But symbolically, notice that the runes in the frame are unreadable, like the conflict over the meaning of words and the Logos in the written words of this chapter. In the commentary Jung says, 'You cry out for the word which has one meaning but no others, so that you escape endless ambiguity' (2009: 270).

In the next image, however, the earth-brown runes are translatable to pictures of posturing human-like figures, while the sky-blue runes remain only suggestive (2009: *LS* 22). In this picture, shown in Plate 15, both the rising and the setting sun are depicted, with Egyptian, Gnostic, and Christian symbols, and the positive golden sun with its sixteen rays, especially positive as the multiple of 4×4 in the symbolism of the quaternity, so important to Jung as the figure of wholeness. Later, the Self is often present in Jung's paintings as a formal, eight-pointed star. Here, the red solar disk is itself no longer the angry, projecting pupil of the eye. Jung says, 'I ate the earth, and drank the sun and became a greening tree that stands alone and grows' (2009: 273). Note that this tree is rooted both above and below, so that its growth seeks the center. Yet at the end of the written part of this chapter, Jung is again in danger of an inflated belief in himself as sun-like. He understands that he must reach for a human hand. But he says, as his painting does, 'I had accepted my darkness,' remembering that this is the acceptance of the rhythm of both day and night (273).

Having depicted the unrelated, sun-drunk world of the Anchorite, in Chapter VI, 'Der Todt,' Jung is free to move fully into the realm of death (2009: *LS* 29). In Plate 16, the monster rising from the underworld sun arouses feelings in us that are almost all that we need to know of the chapter; it is so inhuman, so intent only on its own aggressive voraciousness: it speaks louder than any words. This image, with its primitiveness, is like a child's drawing of his or her own fear. It is also surrounded by toy-like designs of people and crawling creatures. Upon careful examination, each of these contains a child or an egg in utero, and, indeed, in the text, Jung's own death in the dung heap for three days, is notable for the eggs, which hens lay there, waiting as he does for birth/rebirth. This is where the journey leads into 'the undifferentiatable, where none is equal or unequal' (2009: 274). Note its similarity to the alchemical '*prima materia*,' which was not yet the subject of Jung's study.

Chapter VII's painting (Plate 17) is again notable for its tiny wombs, each holding a hooded figure, almost certainly the Kabeiroi, the tiny helpers who are the first-born of earth in several Mediterranean mythologies. They are not toy-like.

In Chapter VIII (Plate 18) Jung once again seeks the differentiated great solar power (2009: *LS* 36). He meets, coming from the east, to seek the declining sun in the west, the giant Izdubar. Izdubar is another name for Gilgamesh, whose Assyrian/Babylonian epic was entitled, in translation, *He Who Sees All.* The tiny figure at the bottom, arms outstretched toward the giant, is Jung. Painted in an ungainly fashion, as a young adolescent might, on Christmas Day, 1915, this arresting figure of Izdubar stands with his feet on the ground, but surrounded by the sky. Also surrounding him, as both a pure design and as symbolic danger, are winged and legged worms, frightening opposites of the winged serpent that always, as Jung says, represents the true union of the opposites in the soul. Equally threatening are the multitudinous crocodiles, like the one in the first painting. Crocodiles are one of the eaters of condemned souls in Egyptian mythology. What at first seem to be Izdubar's own golden wings are really those of the worms, made to seem like his by the ingenuity of the background design. But the wings do become his in a following painting when Izdubar is felled by the poison of the scientific word, the knowledge imparted to him by Jung, that the sun does not really set. 'My own opposite comes toward me and the word of the serpent defeats (him)' (2009: 280). The opposites are still far from integration.

In the painting on page 45 of *Liber Secundus* (Plate 19), we see the first mandala of the book. It is beautiful, communicating the first possibility of wholeness, as Jung, his own feelings torn in empathy for the dying Izdubar, finds that by utilizing the reality of fantasy in both worlds, he is able to contain within an egg the solar hero he has mortally wounded. Here in the painting the egg becomes the golden center of an entire self-cosmos, connected both to Jung's tiny form at the bottom by means of a strange runic figure that is almost representationally human, and by the ever-changing serpent to the transcendent eight-pointed star above, the star that is always Jung's symbol for the Self in *The Red Book.* The folklike motifs of the painting are typically modernist, but the beauty of the painting is all Jung's. The egg is the creative seed of the Orphic creation myth, as well as the possibility of the rebirth of an entire, new, cosmic, and personal reordering.

In order to open the egg of rebirth, Jung utters a series of twelve incantations, each illustrated by a magical painting. These could, again, be the subject of a long paper; here, I can only let one of them speak to us, noting only the celestial sun in its underworld journey, with one of the Kabeiroi steering the boat (Plate 20) (2009: *LS* 55).

On page 64 of *Liber Secundus*, the incantations have proven successful. The egg opens in an elaborate room, and Izdubar/Gilgamesh rises in the painting as the form of fiery energy. In Plate 21, we see the color symbolism of the deep red of the lower sun, represented in the deep-red painting of the carpet; the dark gray-green of the sea; the growing green of the earth on the walls (with the golden celestial sun safely ferried by one of the Kabeiroi past the ferocious Leviathan/Behemoth from the painting on page 55), and a kind of blue-purple energy where the sky might be. Izubar's secured position as earthly solar deity is evident in his own words: 'Where was I? I was completely sun.' In his notes, Shamdasani comments that the legend beneath this painting contains a reference to the ritual of the Vedic fire-healing (2009: 286, note 132).

I will briefly examine the image at the end of Chapter XI (2009: *LS* 71). This image, shown in Plate 22, contains no accompanying text. Here are three snakes, their blue color shimmering with a delicately painted mosaic design, as they coil around one another and the multiple and confusing patterning of the latticework. The star shapes that mark the crossings are four, five, and six pointed as the Self struggles toward the wholeness of the eight-pointed star. The snakes, as most depictions of snakes in this book, have only twisting and curling shapes at either end – impossible, therefore, to know head from tail, the snake energy being always ambiguous. This curled and pointed shape can be observed as a motif throughout the paintings and calligraphy of *The Red Book*, not only directly in the snake images, but also in the serifs of letters, in flames, in abstractly depicted energy forms, and in many other objects. This shape might be termed the leitmotif of this book – the ever-changing, ambiguous, and ambivalent movement that perhaps presages the notion of Hermes in Jung's later work, in its vitality as the force that cannot be finally grasped or fully conceptualized.

From here I move to the most intriguing and mysterious of the paintings in *The Red Book* (2009: *LS* 72). That it precedes the chapter titled 'Hell' makes sense. Hell is the place where Jung cannot blind the eye of the 'evil one,' because good and evil require one another (2009: 290). At this point, they are indicators of a still concrete and preintegrative duality. This painting also precedes the chapter called 'The Sacrificial Murder,' one of the most horrific episodes of the book, entailing Jung's cannibalism of what he would later call the divine child, previously murdered. Through this act Jung is able to recognize and to make the primordial powers a part of himself, where they burn like fire, but prove that God is alive, and that one's 'soul is on remorseless paths' (291).

The cones in this painting (Plate 23) seem to follow the color symbolism of the blue upper world, the green terrestrial world, and the now differentiated celestial sun in an orange-gold color that contrasts with, but is related to, the red sun of the lower world. In a note in *Liber Primus*, Shamdasani observes that the Gnostics expressed the idea that above and below are somehow related by the image of reversed cones and that McGuire saw these shapes also in the upside-down conical shape of Hell and in the heavenly mountain of Dante (2009: 210). The explanation of the cones given in Jung's *Black Book* by the figure Ha are included in two notes by Shamdasani (216, note 205; 291, note 155). Jung does not include these highly esoteric explanations in *The Red Book*.

I would like to add an art-historical note. Earlier, I mentioned the dominant idea of painting prior to modernism (as I am using that term in this essay) – an idea that was presumed to correspond to a single external reality, one of real space seen by a real eye:

> The basic device was the idea of symmetrical . . . cones with one of their apexes the receding vanishing or centric point in the painting, the other the eye of the painter or beholder. Significantly, that eye was singular, conceived in the manner of a lone eye looking through a peep-hole.
>
> (Jay 1988: 6–7)

Both in their relation to the dominant themes of modernism, as well as in their relation to the flatness and lack of perspective in modernist theory, Jung's paintings express their debt to the painting of his time. But more than this, his paintings express in their very being his project to bring both psychic and physical realities into the awareness and being of the individual psyche. Extraordinarily, this image reveals the at least temporary success of that project, bringing both the symbolic and the actual painterly viewpoints literally into visual reality and relationship and, at the same time, superseding them. Perspective, as, much later, both Erwin Panofsky (1971) and Svetlana Alpers (in Jay 1988) would say, has become symbolic.

After this great success, Jung inserts a series of wonderful mandalas, almost as if he needed to strengthen the differentiation in order to continue toward individuation. Only one of these mandalas is shown here in Plate 24 (2009: *LS* 97). A direct communication to us of Jung's own Orphic egg, the upper and lower suns are completely differentiated, their red and gold unmixed, as are the colors of the opposites, all surrounding the eight-pointed star of the Self at the center. What a distance has been traveled from his first sketched mandala in 1917!

Jung, perhaps strengthened by the achievement of direct communication through the mandalas, and by the concomitant possibility of a more stable reordering of the psyche, undergoes in the following chapters (as a whole entitled 'The Divine Folly') the worst of his most personal fears. In this episode of his story, while reading *The Imitation of Christ*, by Thomas à Kempis, Jung is seized and put into an insane asylum.

Here, in this episode of active imagination (2009: *LS* 115), Jung paints an extraordinary and unprecedented image of the Shadow of God, remarkably dwelling within a carefully constructed room in vivid visual perspective (Plate

25). It is, most interestingly, in the form of a *camera obscura*, a dark room with one small aperture through which a tiny amount of focused light comes in, creating an image of outside reality on the opposite wall. This projected image, from the Renaissance to modernism, was considered one of actual and objective reality and was utilized by many artists to help them construct 'correct' perspective. Of course, this could equally well be a film (or today a digital camera), where the light, also focused through the small aperture of a lens, re-creates a picture of what is, again, taken to be 'reality.' Here, the source of the light is the golden celestial sun, which traps the animal-headed shadow. The Shadow of God is part of the split-off Spirit of the Times. He wears the top hat that was a source in *Memories, Dreams, Reflections* of Jung's early vivid fears of death and of the 'Lord Jesus,' who took away dead people with the aid of men in top hats. The secret manikin Jung carved on his pencil box as a child also had a top hat, as Jung magically found a way to own himself (1989: 21–6).

As we come to the end of the 'Divine Folly' chapters, we find a picture of Ama Victu (Plate 26) (2009: *LS* 119). Originally depicted as the Breath of Life, a form of the god spirit that has since become 'the old one,' in this form Ama Victu attempts to eat the sun. A hero figure slays him, this figure being, according to the legend at the bottom of the painting, one of the Kabeiroi, the same one who helped Jung slay Siegfried, the early dream that presaged Jung's attempt to know himself, as recorded in *The Red Book*.

At this cumulative point, Jung inserts another painting (2009: *LS* 125), which resembles the very first image of a village shown at the beginning of the first 'chapter' in *Liber Primus*. This is also similar to the waking vision Jung had as a schoolboy (1989: 80); however, the differences from Jung's first painting are striking. In Plate 27, the vista onto the sea is much wider; many soldiers are guarding the town; and there is much contemporary industrial activity – barges, factories, even contemporary cars and trains belching smoke. The tower with no cross has become a lighthouse. But most startling is the figure, sitting beneath the perfected upper-world golden sun, unified with the red sun of the lower world. The sun spreads energy over all, while the figure itself draws distilled energy from that sun into a feminine vase. This is reminiscent of that same adolescent fantasy of Jung's in *Memories, Dreams, Reflections*, in which he himself could draw an unknown energy down into a tower in the castle keep and have it turn into gold. The figure here, though, is again one of the Kabeiroi, specifically Jung says, the same small dark figure who helped him to kill Siegfried in the dream that initiated the entire project of *The Red Book*. It is the differentiated shadow, related to, but not identical with, either sun.

Finally, as we come to the end of the illustrated portion of *The Red Book*, we are shown (Plate 28) the painting of 'Beloved Philemon' (2009: *LS* 154), the figure from his visions whom Jung considered his guru. Philemon is deliberately painted as an icon. His head and halo replace one of the four symbols of the quaternity, and he is enormous when compared to the scale of his temple in this painting. The snake that winds in all its ambiguous forms throughout this journey is coiled beside him; this time, however, with some small definition to the head, as the ambivalence begins to resolve. Waxing and waning moons are to Philemon's left in the border, and on his right his wing touches what may be a humanized eye. The border encloses him, but the sense of space extends beyond his wings, below his feet, and above his head. He is real, and his reality is more than can be held by the frame. He holds the light of the human self or soul at his heart.

Opposite him is the anima (Plate 29), with the waxing moon beside her and the radiance of something unknown above her (2009: *LS* 155). She is mysterious, and Shamdasani quotes from Jung's study of the Kore, in which Jung describes this image in an impersonal manner, commenting that 'she has taken the place of the altar in church, the place of sacrifice and the receptacle for consecrated relics' (2009: 317, note 283). When Jung, in *Memories, Dreams, Reflections* talks about his building of a miniature church of stones as an adult at the beginning of his long inner journey, he speaks of finding the perfect stone for the church's altar, a red stone, shaped like a perfect four-sided pyramid. It reminded him of the phallus of his childhood dream (1989: 11–12).

Thus far the paintings in *The Red Book* have not afforded very much opportunity to talk of the negative feminine, but the prominence Jung gives to this painting of the anima figure, and the care with which he has executed this painting, especially given the fact that his talent does not seem to have been focused on the figurative, points to several episodes in the book that revolve around the figure of Salome. Around this anima figure moves a group of more or less contemporaneously dressed people, completely individualized, and responding with awe, anger, indifference, and many other feelings to this new element in their church. She is alive but ambiguous, very different from the iconic Philemon with his sagacious face, completely present and wise. Nevertheless we can see her eyes, which are not blind, presaging the ability of the blind Salome (as the character in the text) to see, when Jung is able to accept her love, albeit with a continuing hesitation.

In *Memories, Dreams, Reflections* Jung says of the earthly time covered in *The Red Book:* 'To the extent that I managed to translate the emotions into images – that is to say, to find the images which were concealed in the emotions – I was inwardly calmed and reassured' (1989: 177). The final paintings (Plate 30) are mandalas of great beauty, that 'aesthetic' that Jung refused as the primary point of his circumambulations (2009: *LS* 159). Both refer to the dream he had, probably early in 1927, of being in the city of Liverpool, where it was dark, dreary, and raining (1989: 196–9). He walks through the city to the center, where 'blazing in sunlight' there was a round pool with a little island in the center, and on the island a single magnolia tree: 'the tree stood in the sunlight, and (was) at the same time the source of light.'

From this dream, Jung realized that his ideas of the psychological Self, understood as being at the center of the psyche, were true. 'Through this dream I understood that the Self is the principle and archetype of orientation and meaning.'

The rest of *The Red Book* – including the *Scrutinies* portion, which is without paintings – moves on in its circumambulations and in its sufferings. The last words of *Liber Secundus* are 'The touchstone is being alone with oneself. This is the way' (2009: 330), and the last words of *Scrutinies*, spoken to Philemon by a Shade, are 'I bring you the beauty of suffering. That is what is needed by whoever hosts the worm' (359).

Jung lets us know, in the paintings themselves, that suffering can be transformed into the desire and joy of creativity. Unlike some others of his period of modernism, who relied exclusively either on their art or on their thinking – to name only a few here: Klimt, Nietzsche, von Hofmannsthal, Hölderlin – Jung's vision of a method for alleviating the suffering of human beings in their modernist manifestation led neither to madness nor to surrender. Among other things, as I have tried to indicate, Jung found a center for creativity inside, and perhaps the tiny earthly Kabeiroi outside, that could bring about healing – not a cure for our condition, but a healing of our relation to it.

Touchingly, the handwritten note of 1959, when Jung was in his 84th year and which closes the unfinished *Red Book*, ends on a blank page, with only a single word of an unfinished sentence. That word, in German, is '*Möglichkeit*.' It means 'possibility.'

Note

1 It is important that the sense in which the word *modernism* as used in this essay be understood as referring to the entire period following the consolidation of the Industrial Revolution in the later nineteenth century in Europe and North America and continuing through the twentieth century, at least until the 1950s; after which, the term becomes a matter of critical controversy as applied to the latter half of the century. It is not utilized in this essay to refer to the stylistic modes of the 1920s and the 1930s, as it often is in casual speech. For a clear, if quite conventional, discussion of the term in art history, see the discussion in Part Four, 'The Modern World' in *Janson's History of Art* (revised edition).

References

Davies, Penelope J. E., Denny, Walter B., Hofrichter, Frima Fox, Jacobs, Joseph F., Roberts, Ann M., Simon, David L. (2010) *Janson's History of Art: The Western Tradition*, 8th edn, Upper Saddle River, NJ: Pearson.

Fante, Ake (1986) 'The case of the artist Hilma af Klint,' in Maurice Tuchman (ed.) *The Spiritual in Art: Abstract Painting 1890–1985*, Catalogue for the exhibition of the same name, New York: Abbeville Press.

Hockney, David (2001) *Secret Knowledge: Rediscovering the Techniques of the Old Masters*, London: Thames & Hudson.

Jay, Martin (1988) 'Scopic realms of modernity,' in Hal Foster (ed.), *Vision and Visuality*, Seattle: Bay Press/Dia Foundation.
Morris, William (1882) *Hopes and Fears for Art*, Boston: Roberts Brothers.
Jung, C. G. (1997) *Jung on Active Imagination*, ed. Joan Chodorow, Princeton: Princeton University Press.
—— (1971) *Psychological Types, The Collected Works of C. G. Jung*, vol. 6, Princeton: Princeton University Press.
—— (1953) *Two Essays on Analytical Psychology, The Collected Works of C. G. Jung*, vol. 7, Princeton: Princeton University Press.
—— (1989) *Memories, Dreams, Reflections*, revised edn, New York: Random House.
—— (2009) *The Red Book: Liber Novus*, ed. Sonu Shamdasani, London: W. W. Norton.
Panofsky, Erwin (1971) *Early Netherlandish Painting, Volume One*, New York: Harper & Row.
Sherry, Jay (2011) 'Faint voices from Greenwich Village: Jung's impact on the first American avant-garde,' *Journal of Analytical Psychology*, 56: 692–707.
Von Hofmannsthal, Hugo (2005) *The Lord Chandos Letter and Other Writings*, trans. Joel Rotenberg, New York: New York Review of Books.

6

JUNG'S 'SEVEN SERMONS TO THE DEAD' (1916)

A gnosis for modernity – a multicultural vision of spirituality

Christine Maillard

Jung's *The Red Book* is of great interest to cultural historians for many reasons, but even readers who are quite familiar with Jung may have an uncanny experience reading it. Very different from the rest of the author's work, halfway between autobiography and poetry, *The Red Book* can be understood through the references it makes to various kinds of texts, for instance, to the visionary discourses of certain contemporary esotericists, such as Rudolf Steiner (1861–1925), and to the *fantastique* genre of literature blooming in Europe in the 1910s and 1920s, which depicted processes of initiation.[1]

The Red Book is an account of an individual, personal, but also collective crisis affecting Europe and, in particular, Germanic countries (Pelletier 2008). To understand *The Red Book*, it is necessary to know about the specific period of European culture in which it was written and the specific society of fin-de-siècle Europe (1880–1914), which on the eve of the First World War, saw the emergence of many new artistic trends and the development of deep changes in morals, the rise of political revolutions, and major innovations in the humanities and science.[2] Paradoxically, this period was also experienced as one of decadence and decline, and it ended with the twentieth century's 'seminal catastrophe': the First World War, which plays a key role in *The Red Book*'s *imaginaire* (Jung 2009a, 2009b). The *imaginaire* unfolding in *The Red Book*, for instance, through the representations of femininity or the visions of violence and war, was shared by many actors in that time of social and artistic upheaval. Spiritualism and theosophy also thrived, and the quest for otherness gave a prominent place to India and the Far East (Maillard 2008).

The Red Book is an expression, among others, of those troubled times. It attests to the era's dramatic reconsideration of language and the subject, when the notion of the 'unconscious' acquired a crucial dimension in intellectual life – this crisis of language being, for instance, present in Hugo von

Hofmannsthal's famed *Lord Chandos Letter*, published in 1902 (2000). *The Red Book* also conveys the crisis of values following Nietzsche's writings on the 'transvaluation of all values' and the crisis of religious representations, toward the demise of Christianity and the 'end of religions' foretold by several philosophers.

The Red Book's discourse is different from anything that even the most seasoned readers of all the diverse writings published in its time were used to. In their quest for something to hold on to in order to figure out the meaning of the text, readers naturally turn toward Jung's subsequent theoretical developments. *The Red Book* supposedly constitutes a primary matter of sorts; in the words of Jung himself, a 'prima materia for a lifetime's work' (Jung and Jaffé 1962/1983). Admittedly, a number of works shed some light on the book's meaning, such as the notes of the 1925 seminar, published under the title *Analytical Psychology* (Jung 1989). In that text, Jung explains the main concepts of his psychology of the unconscious, discussing the introspective experience of the years of writing the *Black Books* and *The Red Book*. He precisely mentions several characters that appeared in these imaginary experiences, like Elijah, Salome, and the Snake, and attempts to expand on their psychological significance. *The Red Book*'s discourse is peculiarly distinctive: it alternates between narrative and dialogue, between a visionary style and trivial writing; many characters (humans, animals) occur and later reoccur in another form; and extraordinary, almost unbelievable, phenomena are described. Nevertheless, a few passages stand out from this heterogeneous whole – they appear as oases of coherence and intelligibility.

The 'Seven Sermons to The Dead' and *The Red Book*: pars pro toto

Among these passages, the 'Seven Sermons to the Dead' (*Septem Sermones ad mortuos*) have a specific status in *The Red Book*. As Sonu Shamdasani explains, they were not incorporated in the calligraphic volume, but they were included in the *Scrutinies* (*Prüfungen*), which make up the third and final section of the published text (2009a: 205–6). Composed in 1916, after the main sequences collected in the *Liber Primus* and *Liber Secundus*, the Sermons were, according to Jung himself, written within a few days. For a long time, they were the only visible part of Jung's 'nocturnal' production. Accessible since 1916 (they were initially self-published), the Sermons were appended to the biography-autobiography, *Memories, Dreams, Reflections* (Jung and Jaffé 1962/1983), and they provide a glimpse into that little-known part of Jung's work. The newly published *Red Book* material now allows me to shed more light on this fragment, about which, in the early 1990s, I had written an analysis that highlighted its anticipation of a number of conceptions developed in Jung's psychology of the unconscious and vision of religion (Maillard 1993).[3]

The 'Seven Sermons to the Dead' constitute a very coherent whole within *The Red Book*. They appear to be the longest structured unit in the volume. They echo elements present in other parts of *The Red Book*, while also introducing different and complementary aspects of those elements. Embedded into a quite discontinuous whole, they distill the essence of the message regarding the following aspects: psychology of the unconscious, male and female identity, the hypothesis of the Self, vision of the divine world, and theory of religion. Presented didactically and uttered by the Philemon character, a central figure, they constitute keys to the overall meaning of *The Red Book*. Between each of the Sermons spoken by Philemon, there is a brief exchange between Philemon and the 'I,' which emphasizes the didactic aim of the text; the 'I' is surprised, even offended by Philemon's words, which gives him the opportunity to explain them further (Jung 2009a: *Scrutinies*, 348ff).

Whereas the Sermons shed light on *The Red Book*'s overall intention, the other texts of *The Red Book* allow us to gain a better understanding of the symbolic discourse on which the Sermons are built. This is most specifically the case in the passages in the *Liber Secundus* involving the key figure of Philemon and of the texts collected in *Scrutinies*.[4]

Some major concepts in the *Liber Primus* are not featured in the Sermons per se, but they are implicitly there in a symbolic form: indeed, the notion of the Self (*Selbst*) occasionally appears in the *Liber Primus* and in the *Scrutinies*, and later reappears in the seventh Sermon in the symbolic shape of the Star, 'the goal of man':

> This star is the God and the goal of man.
> This is his one guiding God,
> In him man goes to his rest.
>
> (Jung 2009a: *Scrutinies*, 354)

The links between the 'Seven Sermons to the Dead' and the entire text can also be observed through the protagonists. The Dead themselves, a collective character, are central in the discourse of the *Liber Primus* and the *Liber Secundus;* they appear on several occasions. The Sermons elaborate on their significance: they are 'incomplete' (Jung 2009a: Sermo 3, *Scrutinies*, 350), entities that have not found their destination during their earthly journey. They have not, to use a notion later developed by Jung, gone far enough in their 'individuation' process. In the version published in 1916, the *Seven Sermons to the Dead* were 'told' by Basilides of Alexandria, which seems to root them in the world of historical Gnosticism (Maillard 1993). In *The Red Book*, they are uttered by Philemon, which nuances their general meaning. Among the many characters appearing in the text, Philemon is, indeed, the central and dominant figure in an intellectual paradigm ranging from Ovid's *Metamorphoses* to Goethe's second *Faust.*

In Sermon after Sermon, the Dead's interlocutor, be it Basilides or Philemon, suggests elements to 'complete' the Dead, by having them undergo a sort of sped-up initiation process; one might say, using Jungian terminology from exactly the same period, that Basilides/Philemon introduces the Dead to all the registers of the *transcendent function*[5] by showing them what they have to surrender – one-sidedness (what Jung, in his psychological writings, later called *Einseitigkeit*) – and what they have to achieve – the wholeness of the personality (*Vollständigkeit*). They do this by accepting and integrating the compensatory part, which is also the dark side, in the process of facing the unconscious as Jung himself experienced it.

The 'Seven Sermons to the Dead' and *The Red Book*'s project: A gnosis for modernity

The Red Book's project is linked to all the main themes of Jung's theoretical work and should, therefore, be related to the development of his clinical and hermeneutic notions. The author himself, who saw in the *Liber Novus* the material for a lifetime's work, legitimated reading *The Red Book* in terms of how it anticipates his work to come. Nevertheless, such a reading does not suffice to properly come to terms with *The Red Book*'s meaning; here, I advocate a contextualized reading of *The Red Book*, situating its discourse in relation to others in the same period, and not only based on references to Jung's own work: among the numerous crisis discourses produced in the first third of the twentieth century, *The Red Book* constitutes Jung's own response: his invention of new patterns to exit the crisis based on subverting values and enunciating a gnosis for modernity.

Here, I use 'gnosis' in the sense of a specific form of 'knowledge': the reference to historical Gnosticism, a dissident trend of nascent Christianity, is only one element among others in *The Red Book*'s very rich intertext. *The Red Book*'s project actually relies on a 'fusion' of cultures to be achieved in a new era (symbolized in the text by the Platonic 'new month') (Jung 2009a: *Liber Secundus*, 314). The text is suffused with Jung's multicultural inspiration, from antique cultures to the civilizations of India and the Far East, and his thoughts develop in a constant process of hybridization. 'Fin de siècle' culture was characterized by the interest of many intellectuals in India and the Far East: some of them, like Rudolf Kassner, Rudolf Pannwitz, Hugo von Hofmannsthal, and Hermann Hesse, argued for reassessing Western values in the light of the East (Maillard 2008).

Even before Jung traveled to many countries all over the world, his writings displayed an 'intercultural thought' across civilizations, investigating their differences and their dialogue. Like these other contemporary writers or essayists, he attempted to 'think from outside' (Jullien 2000), from an extra-European point of view, probing into cultural difference to build a psychology with concepts from other cultures, such as the Indian Atman or the Chinese

Tao. This is particularly visible in his seminars, in which he regularly uses notions from Tantrism, Buddhism, and Taoism to shed light on his psychology, as in the Zarathustra Seminar.

Unsurprisingly, *The Red Book* is also informed by intercultural references, some explicit (extra-European myths or texts are mentioned); some implicit through the construction of characters who 'come from the East' (*vom Osten*) (Jung 2009a: *Liber Secundus*, 281), like Izdubar (Gilgamesh) (277, note 97),[6] or like the Indian goddess Kali or the Buddha (*Liber Primus*, 248, 250, note 196, 197; *Liber Secundus*, 277). The *Seven Sermons to the Dead*, in the separately published 1916 version, are addressed to the Dead, who come from 'Alexandria, the city where East and West meet' (Jung 1916). As a literary text, *The Red Book* is based on a 'game' with the cultures of the world, like the one Hermann Hesse would portray in the *Glass Bead Game* a few decades later. The vision of the future, the 'way of the coming man' (*der Weg des Kommenden*) evoked at the beginning of the *Liber Primus*, hinges on this embrace of all cultures in their difference. The theme of welcoming the gods in their diversity, developed through the myth of Philemon and Baucis, is the strongest symbol of this in the text. This multicultural inspiration anchors the subversive conceptions of the work; these conceptions are subversive because they depart from traditional trends. I focus on three aspects:

- The condition of the knowing subject: in its own way, the text raises the Kantian question: What can I know? What are the forms and paths of a nonreductive knowledge?
- The status of religion: How can the downfall of Christianity be explained? What symbolic universe is suited to the man of the present age? What could a 'new religion' be?
- The issue of gendered identity, of relationships between the masculine and the feminine: What is the status of femininity in a world where it is commonly dominated?

The speculations in the 'Sermons' offer their own answers to these questions. Let me sum up the way they unfold.

Sermon 1 is related to Jung's specifically psychological discourse: with the metaphorical terms of 'Pleroma,' 'Creature,' 'quality,' 'difference,' and *principium individuationis*, he introduces the key concepts of the analytical psychology that he would later develop – an original and collective unconscious and its archetypes, the 'I' who hosts consciousness – and he establishes the dialectical process of the 'I' and the unconscious also formulated further in the 1916 text on the *transcendent function* and studied in depth in *The Relation between the I and the Unconscious* (Jung 1928/1966).

Sermons 2 to 4 present a system of the divine world that initially seems quite peculiar, in which negative theology, polytheism, and the question of evil in the form of the Devil all play a significant role. They explore major themes of Jung's religious thought, expressed two or three decades later in *Answer to Job*, in his essay on the symbolic meaning on the Trinity, and in the writings collected in the *Aion* volume (Jung 1951).

Sermons 5 and 6 revolve around polarities – the celestial and the chthonian, the masculine and the feminine, the sexual and the spiritual – and echo the writings on animus and anima, the *Psychology of Transference*, and the hermeneutics of alchemy that Jung elaborated on in the 1940s and 1950s. The idea of *coniunctio*, a key concept in Jung's later psychology, as well as the conditions necessary to achieve it, already emerge here.

Lastly, Sermon 7, constructed around the symbol of the Star, is a discourse on the 'ideal,' or perfected, stage of the individual entity, of the Self.

The 'Seven Sermons to the Dead' are, in many respects, the source of Jung's oeuvre: most of the main mythologems and symbols found in the Sermons reappear in Jung's later clinical and metapsychological work, fleshed out and integrated into conceptual developments (Maillard 1993). The text is a poetic meditation on the transformation of the individual entity, in a process Jung later called 'individuation' – becoming oneself, reaching the Self, which occurs through the experience of facing the unconscious and shifting psychological structures that displace the center of gravity of life and relationships.

Knowing the 'Depths'

The opposition between 'spirit of this time' and 'spirit of the depths' ('*Geist dieser Zeit*/*Geist der Tiefe*') is outlined in the first pages of the *Liber Primus* and is fundamental to the question of knowledge as Jung raises it in *The Red Book*, positing the possibility of another source of knowledge than the prevailing ones (2009a: *Liber Primus*, 229ff). From this perspective, the 'Seven Sermons to the Dead' are informed by this 'spirit of the depths': the knowledge they provide has a compensatory function – a key concept in Jung's work – in relation to the 'spirit of this time.' They assert another possible approach to knowledge than scientific approaches, which are criticized in *The Red Book* (*Liber Primus*, 264). This symbolic knowledge relies on taking into account 'sense' (*Sinn*), but also 'non-sense' (*Widersinn*, literally what goes 'against sense,' that is, products of the unconscious that initially do not seem to make sense), from the interaction between the two results 'hyper-sense' (*Übersinn*).[7] Such thinking in binary oppositions transcended by a third term is typical of Jung's work.

What is at stake here is a new cognitive attitude, through which what is usually overlooked emerges: the interlocutors of the *I* in *The Red Book*, emanating from this spirit of the depths, are in charge of expressing this new position, this knowledge that is not conveyed through concepts or ideas, but through symbols. Several passages in *The Red Book* expand on the definition of 'symbol':

> The symbol is the word that goes out of the mouth, that one does not simply speak, but that rises out of the depth of the self as a word of power and great need and places itself unexpectedly on the tongue. It is an astonishing and perhaps seemingly irrational word, but one recognizes it as a symbol since it is salient to the conscious mind. If one accepts the symbol, it is as if a door opens leading into a new room whose existence one previously did not know.
>
> (Jung 2009a: *Scrutinies*, 311)

The central figure Philemon, who utters the 'Seven Sermons to the Dead,' is an Old Wise Man, whose teachings are concerned with this symbolic form of knowledge. Asserting the validity of this form of knowledge is unusual during a period in civilization when science has progressed and positivism has thrived, that is, in the second half of the nineteenth century during Jung's formative years. The text was also conceived in the wake of the dispute with Freud on the interpretation of the unconscious through sexuality only and establishes spirituality as a counterpoint.

In his psychology of culture, Jung studied models derived from the traditions of European esotericism (Maillard 2005): they are present throughout his work and are a major source of inspiration to him. He strived to understand phenomena that rationality alone did not allow to comprehend, from alchemy to astrology or paranormal phenomena. He also examined some of the most significant facets of the history of this tradition, studying, for instance, Paracelsus, the physician and philosopher (Jung 1929; 1941/1942; 1942), and reading Swedenborg, the visionary savant who, as he did, made use of the two discourses, that of reason and that of the depths.

The dialogue portions in the first two Sermons elaborate on this opposition between 'believing' and 'knowing' ('*Glauben*' and '*Wissen*'). 'Believing' here refers to an obsolete attitude, a defeat of thought. Like the remainder of *The Red Book*, the 'Seven Sermons to the Dead' suggest a 'third way' that differs from believing and from purely instrumental knowledge. This move on Jung's part results in a new vision of what a religion of the future could be.

A new religious era: against the tyranny of the single god, polytheism

The Red Book and, to an even greater extent, the 'Seven Sermons to the Dead' contain a discourse on religion that involves two core ideas:

- A new religious era is dawning
- Polytheism as a fundamental value and as a model

The idea of a new religious idea is present in all of Jung's work and distinguishes his project from Freud's, who saw religion as an obscurantist impasse. Jung later asserted the presence of a 'religious function' in the human psyche, enduring regardless of the changes affecting civilization or society. The image of a new 'month' in the great year, alluding to a Platonic temporality, is a recurrent one in *The Red Book* (Jung 2009a: *Liber Secundus*, 314): it introduces an era when attitudes toward religion change, although it is not the end of religion. Nietzsche's 'death of God' is here replaced by the advent of a new form of religious experience, involving a new image of the divine, the symbolic birth of a new god.

The discourse of *The Red Book* on religion first describes the crisis of Christian religious representations, a critique often voiced in the context of early twentieth-century European civilization and shared by many intellectuals. The critique of Christianity in the 'Seven Sermons to the Dead' starts with the question of the 'death of God,' a question that the Dead ask Philemon at the beginning of the text. Then follows a long discourse on Christianity's divine image:

> [. . .] The dead drew near and lined the walls and cried out:
> 'We want to know about God. Where is God? Is God dead?'
> But Philemon rose and said: 'God is not dead. He is alive as ever.'
>
> (Jung 2009a: *Scrutinies*, 348)

This critique essentially targets monotheism, seen as an unbearable reduction of the divine (Sermo IV) (351), and the conception of God as *summum bonum* – as a supreme being deprived of an evil dimension, which, according to Jung, stems from an ontological minimization of evil (*privatio boni*) (Jung 1952/1967). Why criticize monotheism, however?

> Happy am I who can recognize the multiplicity and diversity of the Gods. But woe unto you, who replace this incompatible multiplicity with a single God. In so doing you produce the torment of incomprehension and mutilate the creation whose nature and aim is differentiation.
>
> (2009a: *Scrutinies*, 351)

Seen from a psychological standpoint, the monotheistic choice excludes everything that makes life rich and diverse; it is a 'monotono-theism' in the sense of Nietzsche, amputating the psyche's unconscious side. The Jungian critique of this mutilating monotheism and his call for what Jungian research later called 'polytheism of the soul' reaches its apex in the 'Seven Sermons to the Dead' with the representation of the supreme God Abraxas, featured in the entirety of Sermon 3. This God is both the great creator and the great destroyer, assuming in himself the opposite roles of the major divinities of Hinduism, Vishnu and Shiva, who, respectively, maintain and destroy the universe created by Brahma. Abraxas both creates and destroys what he has created; he is both good and fearsome, also like the Nietzschean Dionysos:

> Abraxas produces truth and lying, good and evil, light and darkness, in the same word and in the same act. Therefore Abraxas is terrible.
> [. . .]
> He is the fullness that seeks union with emptiness.
> (Jung 2009a: *Scrutinies*, 350)

This critical vision of Christian representations comes with an alternative proposition, another vision of the divine world, one based on a polytheistic theology, on the notion of the ambivalence of the divine, and the reintegration of the Devil into the divine world. These three features of the theological universe in 'Seven Sermons to the Dead' are obviously linked to Jung's reception of Nietzsche. But they are also rooted in Jung's multicultural experience, in his interest in Indian or Indian-born religions: characters from the words of Hinduism and Buddhism appear in the discourse of *The Red Book*. The figure of Salome, who is linked to the Judeo-Christian world, is said to be identical to the Indian goddess Kali (Jung 2009a: *Liber Primus*, 250, note 196), a menacing figure in charge of destruction. As historians have attested, Jung had acquired the entire collection of Max Muller's *Sacred Books of the East* (*Liber Secundus*, 285, note 130). Jung's thoughts on religion also take into account the 'variety of religious experience' (William James, 1902), and this multicultural approach later provides the basis for Jung's theory of archetypes – the symbolic structures found in all civilizations and rooted in the human mind's disposition to produce symbols. Jung's extra-European inspiration makes itself particularly felt in this vision of the divine world outlined in the 'Sermons.' Thus, it is necessary to turn toward India to understand what the 'polytheistic' idea means to Jung.

Subverting gendered identities

There may be fewer feminine figures than masculine ones in *The Red Book*, but feminine figures are important ones. Aside from Philemon, the Soul is the main character who interacts with the I, and she appears as a woman. The character of Salome, who is together with the prophet Elijah, is the other major feminine figure. As noted, in *The Red Book* the Jewish Salome is associated, in a typical Jungian gesture of cultural hybridization, with the Indian Kali, a fearsome goddess with the power to create and destroy, a 'Great Goddess' (Jung 2009a: *Liber Primus*, 248). In the 'Seven Sermons to the Dead,' a text pervaded by symbols, femininity as a principle and as a structure and its tense relationship with the masculine plays an important part: 'Spirituality conceives and embraces. It is womanlike and therefore we call it MATER COELESTIS, the celestial mother. Sexuality engenders and creates. It is manlike, and therefore we call it PHALLOS, the earthly father' (*Scrutinies*, 352).

Here, the conception of femininity is chiefly based on reversing the values generally attributed to the masculine and the feminine in the Western tradition, where the spirit is considered as masculine and matter or nature as feminine. Instead, spirituality is said to be 'womanlike': the text goes beyond the clichés on the representation of the feminine as 'nature,' matter, in opposition to the masculine world of 'culture' or of the spirit. What is remarkable is the equal relationship between the two gendered principles: each has their role, and neither is subordinate to the other. Following the dominant categories in the society of the time, here, the feminine principle, as it is related to spirituality, even prevails over the masculine principle.

This subversion of the conception of femininity remains constantly present in Jung's work after the 'Seven Sermons to the Dead,' with the theoretical model he develops within the framework of his theory of archetypes from 1918: the animus and the anima, archetypes of the inner masculine and feminine, which take into account the bipolarity of the individual's psyche. With the theory of animus, the woman's inner masculinity, and anima, the man's inner feminine imago, Jung develops a theory accounting for the complexity of individual psychology and the relations between genders. It is a speculative theory, but one that is rooted in the analytical experience and in the analysis and interpretation of images appearing in patients' dreams and products of imagination. Rather than conceiving of gendered identities as a binary polarity, Jung sees them as a structure with four terms – a dynamic one, based on something other than alternative: the masculine and its anima (inner femininity), and the feminine and its animus (inner masculinity). Here, femininity is the masculine's alterity, like the Other, but not as the dark side of the psyche – a long-term conception that led to women being diabolized, as in the witch hunts during the late Middle Ages in Europe – but rather as a form of spiritual otherness, conveying the spirit's dimension.

For these conceptions of femininity as a powerful force, Jung drew inspiration from a Swiss author, also from Basel, Johann Jakob Bachofen (1815–87), who developed a theory of matriarchy, positing that there had been a time in civilization when women held power. His main book, *Das Mutterrecht* (*The Matriarchy*, 1861), explores what he calls gynaecocracy, the political and social power held by women in ancient societies. Jung took much interest in civilizations in which the feminine principle played a central role, as representation, including in religion and specifically in India. It is well known that in Brahmanism (Hinduism), there is a pantheon with multiple divinities in which female divinities have male consorts. The goddess Kali, one of Hinduism's major representations, embodies aspects of femininity that are missing from the Western collective consciousness. Jung also makes references to other Eastern cultural areas, such as Taoism, in which the masculine and feminine principles are present on a cosmic level through the alternation of the yin and the yang.

In the Western world, far from the prevailing trends, Jung also found alternative models of femininity, as they appear in Gnosticism and alchemy. He reinterprets Western civilization, showing that the feminine principle had an impact on an occult level, outside of dominant trends, precisely in these doctrines of Western esotericism.

The notion of gender equality is a fundamental one: each of the two genders equally participates in achieving the alchemical opus, the ultimate goal being the redemption of matter, and, from a psychological point of view, the realization of the Self based on unconscious material.

Arguably the most important representation of femininity in Jung's work is that of Sophia, divine wisdom, which is present in Gnosticism and in the writings of the mystic Jacob Böhme. As a representation of femininity, Sophia differs from the Virgin Mary, mother of God; she is a feminine Holy Spirit of sorts. The term *sophiology* is used whenever femininity is associated with soteriological or eschatological motifs. These representations of a celestial and spiritual femininity are at the core of Jung's psychology. He developed a 'sophiology,' or theory of feminine wisdom, different from the one derived from the masculine principle.

But in Christian representations themselves, Jung observed a discourse on spiritual femininity: he saw the Assumption of the Virgin, the dogma declared by Pius XII in 1950, as a significant step, the sign of a new religious era, that of the Holy Spirit, according to the prophetic vision of the Calabrian monk Joachim of Fiore on the three ages of humanity: the era of the Father, of the Son, and that, still to come, of the Holy Spirit.[8] Jung, a Joachimite and thus an esoteric Christian, places the representation of the Trinity at the center of his interpretation of Christianity; to him, this key dogma constitutes the essential part of the Christian message (Jung 1995: GW 18/2, par. 1652ff). He was, therefore, particularly interested in the representations of the feminine as a part of the Trinity, which so becomes a quaternity.

For Jung, the dogma of the Assumption of Mary was the sign of a move beyond the exclusively patriarchal stage in the representation of the divine and the announcement of the reintegration of the feminine principle in the divine world. He saw in it a great symbol, a momentous event in collective consciousness, the sign that this new dawn was near, or had even already occurred. Jung perceived religious evolution as a series of exclusions and reintegrations and the feminine as one of the objects of this process. Others, such as the principle of evil, are also due to be reintegrated after a millennium of exclusion. And this is yet another key theme in *The Red Book*: 'You are entirely unable to live without evil' (Jung 2009a: *Liber Secundus*, 287).

Notes

1 For example, Gustav Meyrink's literary work: *The Golem* (1913/1915), *The Green Face* (1917), *The White Dominican* (1921), and *The Angel of the West Window* (1927).

2 On fin de siècle-culture in Germany, see Haupt (2008), Facos (2003), Strathausen (2003), and Lubkoll (2002).

3 See also Stefan Hoeller's *The Gnostic Jung and the Seven Sermons to the Dead* (1985) and Robert Segal's *The Gnostic Jung*, including 'Seven Sermons to the Dead' (1992).

4 *The Red Book*'s Appendix C, which reproduces a sketch written by Jung on 16 January 1916, goes in a similar direction.
5 See the eponymous essay written in 1916, the same year Jung wrote the Sermons (*The Transcendent Function* [*Die transzendente Funktion*] 1916/1958).
6 Izdubar is said to be 'The Hero from the East.'
7 For a critical approach to Shamdasani's translation of 'supreme meaning' for 'Übersinn,' see Giegerich (2010).
8 On Joachim of Fiore and his cultural impact, see Henri de Lubac, *La postérité spirituelle de Joachim de Flore* (1987); Marjorie Reeve, *Joachim of Fiore & the Prophetic Future* (1999); and Marjorie Reeve and Warwick Gould, *Joachim of Fiore and the Myth of the Eternal Evangel in the Nineteenth Century* (1987).

References

Bachofen, Johann Jakob (1861) *Das Mutterrecht. Eine Untersuchung über die Gynaikokratie der alten Welt nach ihrer religiösen und rechtlichen Natur*, Stuttgart: Krais & Hoffmann.

Facos, Michelle (ed.), (2003) *Art, Culture, and National Identity in Fin-de-Siècle Europe*, Cambridge: Cambridge University Press.

Giegerich, Wolfgang (2010) '*Liber Novus*, that is, The New Bible: A First Analysis of C. G. Jung's *Red Book*,' *Spring: A Journal of Archetype and Culture*, 83 (Spring): 361–411.

Haupt, Sabine (ed.) (2008) *Handbuch Fin de Siècle*, Stuttgart: Kröner.

Hoeller, Stefan (1985) *The Gnostic Jung and the Seven Sermons to the Dead*, Wheaton, IL: Chiron Press.

James, William (1902) *The Varieties of Religious Experience: Being a Study in Human Nature*, New York: Longmans, Green & Co.

Jullien, François (2000) *Penser d'un dehors (La Chine): entretiens d'Extrême-Occident*, entretien avec Thierry Marchaisse, Paris: Le Seuil.

Jung, C. G. (1995) 'Anwort auf einen Brief von Reverend David Cox,' in C. G. Jung *Gesammelte Werke*, vol. 18/2, Olten/Freiburg im Breisgau: Walter-Verlag.

—— (1916) *Septem Sermones ad Mortuos*: 'Die sieben Belehrungen der Toten. Geschrieben von Basilides in Alexandria, der Stadt, wo der Osten den Westen berührt,' Self-published.

—— (1916/1958) *Die transzendente Funktion* [*The Transcendent Function*], in C. G. Jung, *Die Dynamik des Unbewussten, Gesammelte Werke*, vol. 8, Olten/Freiburg im Breisgau: Walter-Verlag.

—— (1928/1966) *Die Beziehungen zwischen dem Ich und dem Unbewussten* [*The Relations Between the I and the Unconscious*], in C. G. Jung, *Zwei Schriften über analytische Psychologie, Gesammelte Werke*, vol. 7, Olten/Freiburg im Breisgau: Walter-Verlag, (1964/1974).

—— (1929) *Paracelsus* and (1941/1942) *Paracelsus als Arzt*, in C. G. Jung, *Gesammelte Werke*, vol. 15, Olten/Freiburg im Breisgau: Walter-Verlag.

—— (1942) *Paracelsus als geistige Erscheinung*, in C. G. Jung, *Gesammelte Werke*, vol. 13, Olten/Freiburg im Breisgau: Walter-Verlag.

—— (1951) *Aion, Untersuchungen zur Symbolgeschichte*, in C. G. Jung, *Gesammelte Werke*, vol. 9/2, Olten/Freiburg im Breisgau: Walter-Verlag.

—— (1952/1967) *Antwort auf Hiob* [Answer to Job (1952)], in C. G. Jung, *Zur Psychologie westlicher und östlicher Religion, Gesammelte Werke*, vol. 11, Olten/Freiburg im Breisgau: Walter-Verlag.

—— (1988) *Nietzsche's Zarathustra. Notes of the Seminar Given in 1934–1939*, ed. James L. Jarrett, 2 vol., Princeton: Princeton University Press 1988.
—— (1989) *Analytical Psychology: Notes on the Seminar Given in 1925*, ed. William McGuire, Princeton: Bollingen Series, Princeton University Press.
—— (2009a) *The Red Book: Liber Novus*, ed. Sonu Shamdasani, trans. Mark Kyburz, John Peck, and Sonu Shamdasani, New York: W. W. Norton and Co.
—— (2009b) *Das Rote Buch. Liber Novus*, Düsseldorf: Patmos.
Jung C. G., and Jaffé, Aniela (1962/1983) *Memories, Dreams, Reflections*, trans. Richard and Clara Winston, London: Flamingo.
Lubac, Henri de (1987) *La postérité spirituelle de Joachim de Flore*, 2 vols, Paris: Lethielleux.
Lubkoll, Christine (ed.) (2002) *Das Imaginäre des Fin de Siècle*, Freiburg im Breisgau: Rombach (Originally published Rombach Wissenschaft: Reihe Litterae, 1988.)
Maillard, Christine (1993) *Les Sept Sermons aux Morts de Carl Gustav Jung*, Nancy: Presses universitaires de Nancy.
—— (2005) 'C. G. Jung' in Jean-Pierre Brach, Antoine Faivre, Wouter J. Hanegraaff (eds), *Dictionary of Gnosis and Western Esotericism*, vol. 2, 648–53, Leiden: E. J. Brill.
—— (2008) *L'Inde vue d'Europe. Histoire d'une rencontre (1750–1950)*, Paris: Albin Michel.
Pelletier, Nicole (ed.) (2008) *Crises et conscience de crise dans les pays de langue allemande (années vingt et trente)*, Bordeaux: Presses universitaires de Bordeaux.
Reeve, Marjorie (1999) *Joachim of Fiore & the Prophetic Future: A Medieval Study in Historical Thinking*, Gloucester: Alan Sutton Publishing.
Reeve, Marjorie and Gould, Warwick (1987) *Joachim of Fiore and the Myth of the Eternal Evangel in the Nineteenth Century*, Oxford: The Clarendon Press.
Segal, Robert (ed.) (1992) *The Gnostic Jung*, including 'Seven Sermons to the Dead,' Princeton: Princeton University Press.
Shamdasani, Sonu (2009) Introduction to *The Red Book. Liber Novus*, ed. Sonu Shamdasani, New York/London: Norton.
Strathausen, Carsten (2003) *The Look of Things: Poetry and Vision around 1900*, University of North Carolina Studies in the Germanic Languages and Literatures, vol. 126, Chapel Hill: University of North Carolina Press.
Von Hofmannsthal, Hugo (2000) *Ein Brief*, in Hugo von Hofmannsthal *Der Brief des Lord Chandos: Schriften zur Literatur, Kultur und Geschichte*, ed. Mathias Mayer, Stuttgart: Reclam.

7

'THE WEALTH OF THE SOUL EXISTS IN IMAGES'

From medieval icons to modern science

George Hogenson

The publication of *The Red Book* or *Liber Novus* presents the reader with a complex and rather daunting hermeneutical challenge. In an early commentary Wolfgang Giegerich questions its very status as a book that can be seen as 'part of Jung's oeuvre.' *The Red Book*, Giegerich argues, is 'a most curious and puzzling phenomenon' (Giegerich 2010: 362). My own effort to define a point of entry for thinking about *The Red Book* begins with the first line of Jung's own narrative, following his citations from Isaiah and the Gospel of John, 'If I speak in the spirit of this time, I must say: no one and nothing can justify what I must proclaim to you' (Jung 2009: 229b). Is *Liber Novus*, in fact, a proclamation?

The philosopher of religion, Paul Ricoeur, examines the nature of proclamation in an important essay where he distinguishes between 'a hermeneutic . . . where the accent is placed on speech and writing,' emphasizing the historical significance of the founding of a tradition in which the interpretation of the tradition is itself part of the tradition, and what he terms a hermeneutic of the sacred that shows itself in the form of a phenomenology of manifestation (1995). I argue that we do not encounter a proclamation, as Jung encounters his soul in the opening pages of *Liber Primus*, but rather precisely this phenomenology of manifestation in the form of the valorization of the image, as in Jung's expression that provides the title for this chapter, 'The wealth of the soul exists in images' (Jung 2009: 232). Citing Kant's *Critique of Judgment*, Ricoeur casts a light on why this simple line in Jung orients us toward manifestation and a moment in the phenomenology of the sacred:

> [In the Critique of Judgment], in speaking of aesthetic ideas, Kant related them to the productive imagination that, he says, 'gives us more to think about' (par. 49) because the capacity to determine an object by a concept is surpassed by the capacity to present the ideas

> of our reason in images. The sacred is in the same position in relation to its manifestations as the ideas of our reason are in Kant in relation to their presentation in the products of the imagination. Or, to use an expression of Henri Corbin, we could say that the sacred unfolds a space of manifestation that must be called imaginary (imaginal) rather than logical in nature.
>
> (1995: 50)

Ricoeur's distinction between proclamation and manifestation provides, I believe, an orienting structure not only for understanding Jung's relation to his experience but also to the larger context within which he was working. In the first instance, Ricoeur allows us to begin orienting ourselves to Jung's medieval, premodern understanding of the image and its relationship to knowledge – *scientia* – as well as, ironically, questions about the rise of the modern scientific model by which we understand the world and our place in it. Secondarily, we can also see how Jung's approach to the image presents a stark contrast to Freud's conception of the nature of the psyche and the relationship between word and image. To be clear on this point before proceeding further, I do not believe one can read *Liber Novus* without taking account of Jung's relationship to Freud and the nature of the conflict that engulfed them.

Briefly outlined, both Freud and Jung confronted the same problem in establishing their systems of psychology: how to move from deeply subjective experiences to generalizations regarding the nature of the psyche. In his famous letter to Fliess of 15 October 1897, where Freud first lays out his argument regarding the Oedipus drama, he is clearly trying to establish the grounds for the generalization of his own introspective investigations (Masson 1985: 272). One can almost, but not quite, construct a syllogism out of Freud's 'discovery': *All people react strongly to Sophocles' play; I react strongly to the play and realize through introspection that I harbor the same impulses; therefore, all people harbor the same impulses because they react strongly to the play.* Freud realized, I believe, that a pseudo-syllogism such as this could not carry the weight of his argument, and therefore, he had to find other means by which to establish the universality of his model. This led Freud, as Patricia Kitcher has demonstrated in great detail (1995), to embrace a variety of nineteenth-century scientific propositions and theories that were, unfortunately for Freud, being rapidly replaced by new theoretical developments in all of the sciences Freud was referencing. Most important among Freud's scientific misappropriations was his embrace of Lamarckism, or the inheritance of acquired characteristics. In *Totem and Taboo*, Freud deployed a Lamarckian approach to evolution to underwrite his notion that a primal event, the struggle between a father and his sons for possession of the tribal females, would answer the question of why the division between consciousness and the unconscious exists in the first place and also why human beings have inherited this characteristic. Jean Laplanche and Jean-Bertrand Pontalis remark in their invaluable *The Language of Psychoanalysis* that Freud's argument is the founding myth of psychoanalysis (1973). At the same time that Freud was writing *Totem and Taboo*, Jung was producing *Symbols and Transformations of the Libido*. Although Jung recounts in *Memories, Dreams, Reflections* that it was the last section of this book – 'The Sacrifice' – that provided the final nail in the coffin of his relationship with Freud, Jung was also proposing a radically different 'myth' of the psyche's origin. Whereas Freud was intent on vindicating the foundational role of repression within his system, Jung took the opposite position and proposed that the central function of the unconscious was projection. Whereas Freud argued for what he called 'primal repression' – *Urverdrängung* – Jung, as I have previously argued (Hogenson 1983), proposed a vision of what I termed 'primal projection.' What is important about this dispute is that in both cases the so-called primal element in each system provides the basis for the constitution of a world of the psyche, which led me to argue that both Freud and Jung should be seen as cosmogonists.

In the early portions of *Liber Secundus*, precisely this 'cosmogonic distinction' emerges as Jung engages Armonius the Anchorite in a provocative discussion of the relationship of the word to the incarnation and the first verses of the Gospel of John (Jung 2009: 268b–9a). The discussion with the Anchorite focuses Jung's attention on a reversal of his assumptions about the Gospel, as the Anchorite argues that in John, the Logos is actually raised up to the human, rather than the human being subordinated to the Logos. The Anchorite is clear that he has 'learned to see that John has in fact done the great service of bringing the meaning of the ΛΟΓΟΣ up to man' (269a).[1] This exchange is embedded in a discussion of the influence Philo Judeaus may have had on the writer of the Gospel. For Philo, the argument goes, the word would have had priority over the human. The significance of this exchange, however, derives its weight from Jung's initial presentation of his position regarding the status of the image in relation to the word. My reason for saying this is the way in which Jung begins *The Red Book* with a set of invocations of the image. By the time Jung has reached the third paragraph of his text, the status of the image for understanding this book has been established by the association of the image with the *übersinn*, translated here as 'supreme meaning.' The resonances with Nietzsche's concept of the *Übermensch* are self-evident, but as the philosopher Gianni Vattimo remarked, 'The problem of what Nietzsche means with his concept of the *Übermensch* lies entirely in how we understand the prefix *über*' (Vattimo 2006: 83).[2] The same issue arises with Jung's notion of the *übersinn*. The *übersinn*, we are told, derives from the 'melting together of sense and nonsense,' as prescribed by the 'spirit of the depths' (Jung 2009: 229b), and is further defined by its relationship to the image:

> *But the supreme meaning is the path, the way and bridge to what is to come. That is the God yet to come. It is not the coming God himself, but*

The medieval moment in Jung

In the concluding paragraph of the draft portion of *Liber Secundus*, Jung locates himself in relation to a point of origin for addressing the image: 'I must catch up with a piece of the Middle Ages – within myself. We have only finished the Middle Ages of – others. I must begin early, in that period when the hermits died out' (2009: 330b). Earlier in the book, Jung had already alerted the reader to the importance of the early medieval period for understanding his project and had provided something of a guide to where we should look. 'To find their soul,' he writes on page 236a, 'the ancients went into the desert. This is an image. The ancients lived their symbols, since the world had not yet become real for them.'[3] In the case of the image, one critical point in the early Middle Ages is the early eighth century, when Leo III, emperor in the East, precipitated the iconoclastic controversy (Moran 1989). In condemning the use of images, Leo took a decisive step in the history of Christianity, one that would return in various forms for the next thousand years or more. Needless to say, Leo had ancient grounds for forbidding the use of images in the Mosaic prohibition on graven images. Leo proceeded, however, without consulting the other branch of the Christian church in the person of Pope Gregory II, for whom images retained a useful role for the instruction of the illiterate (Diebold 2000). Further conflict ensued, with the argument moving back and forth between iconoclasts and iconophiles until the Ecumenical Council of Nicaea in 787 declared the validity of images, a decision that was reinforced by a subsequent council in 843.

In an important essay, 'The Prototype and the Image,' concerning these events and their consequences, the philosopher of religion Jean-Luc Marion argues for the intimate relationship between the icon and what Jung would call the archetype in itself:

> Whereas in imitation, the more the derived image is perfected, the less it depends upon the glory of its model, to the point that the tangential autarchy of the glory inevitably drives it to the self-reference of an idol, the icon, on the contrary, glorifies itself only by returning all glory to the invisible. Iconoclasm criticizes the supposed idolatrous derivation of icons, because it persists in interpreting according to the logic of similitude and mimetic rivalry, without ever suspecting – or accepting – that the *typos* has categorically broken away from any imitation of an original. The icon does not represent; it presents – not in the sense of producing a new presence (as in a painting) but in the sense of making present the holiness of the Holy One.
>
> (2004: 76f)

Murray Stein also cites this essay, commenting on Marion's discussion of the icon, writing, 'In Jungian terms, the icon is a symbol, which mediates the unknown and otherwise invisible reality of the psyche to the conscious ego. The symbol makes the archetype available to consciousness' (2008: 321, note 13). We are, then, by moving to the early medieval period, on the threshold of Jung's theory of archetypes. To the degree that this is the case, we should look at the relationship between the image and the archetype as it was seen in this period. The foremost intellectual force in the Christian west at this time was John Scottus Eriugena (800–77), an Irish monk active in France and, importantly, able to read Greek and therefore able to access texts in the Greek tradition. Durmot Moran, in his detailed study of Eriugena, highlights the consequences of having a Latin rite cleric responding to the Greek tradition:

> It is clear that Eriugena develops [his] view of the interchangeability of God and perfect human nature based on his interpretation of Greek Christology (which affirmed the cosmic humanity of Jesus) and on the implications of accepting the concept of deification or theosis. Deification is usually interpreted in the Latin Church as involving only the increasing similarity between human nature and God, a polishing of the image, as it were, until human nature attains likeness to God. They stop short of claiming that this image can become perfectly identical with the archetype in all respects. Eriugena, however, has no qualms about defining a perfect image as one which has all features in common with the archetype – to the same degree of perfection as is found in the archetype.
>
> (1989: 169)

Jung relies less on Eriugena than he does on Meister Eckhart and Nicholas of Cusa – who actually stands at the end of the Middle Ages – for insight. But both Eckhart and Cusanus hold positions that are similar to Eriugena – Cusanus interestingly was also able to read Greek and had participated in a Papal mission to the leaders of the Orthodox Church. Still, Eckhart, while using a somewhat more modern philosophical language, takes a position on the status of the image that is very close to Eriugena's. 'An image' Eckhart writes, 'is not of itself; nor is it for itself. It has its origin in that of which it is the image . . . An image receives its being from that of which it is the image. It is one being with it and it is the same being' (Schürmann 1978: 94).

There was a problem with this position, however, that was already appearing in the early medieval period that sheds some light on the Freud/Jung controversy, as well as illuminates the larger issue of the status of the archetype in Jungian theory: the problem of translation for those who, unlike Eriugena, did not read Greek. Reiner Schürmann, in his essential study of Heidegger's philosophy of action, points to a fundamental difference in the Greek and Latin forms of the issue of archetypes that will have resonance with Jungian theory:

> The complementary notion to *archē* is *telos*; that to 'principle' is something entirely different, namely the sequent, the consequence, the derivative, the 'issue.' As the concept of origin changes its linguistic milieu, it also changes its strategy . . . [To] say *principium* instead of *archē* is to extend the order of derivatives beyond the simple case of substance and accidents. In this way, the 'principle' comes to designate the supreme cause of all things . . . Two key texts especially testify to the transition toward order: the first paragraphs of Duns Scotus's [1265–1308] *Treatise on God as First Principle* and a few short paragraphs in Leibniz's *Monadology*. At the medieval apogee of Latin thought in Scotus, the order derived from a first is an order of entities receiving their cohesion from the divine substance; at the close of the Latin epoch in Leibniz, it is an order of propositions receiving their coherence from human subjectivity.
>
> (1987: 107)

It is at this point, Schürmann argues, that the world becomes an-archic – the prelude to the death of God and the end of metaphysics. I believe Schürmann also sheds light on the difficulty Freud had comprehending Jung, as remarked on by Lacan previously, insofar as the linguistic hermeneutic would emphasize the internal logic of a proposition; it would fall into the realm of the *principium*, rather than the *archetype*. It is precisely at this juncture between archetype and image, as distinct from principle and discourse, that we can take the turn promised in the title of this paper from medieval spirituality to modern science.

Ironically, it is the last of the great medieval philosophers who sets the stage for the development of modern science. In his dialogue, *De Idiota*, Cusanus (1401–64) proposes that the common shopkeeper, with his balance scale, is in a better position to interpret the world than the learned philosopher. As the common man leads the philosopher toward greater understanding, it becomes evident that measurement will become the guiding principle – that word again – for the sciences. Cusanus was, in fact, the first to decenter the earth and dispute the Aristotelian view of the perfection of the cosmos. Nicolaus Copernicus and Johannes Kepler revered him, relying on his insights to guide their own speculations. Gottfried Wilhelm von Leibniz, who was influenced by Cusanus, in many respects stands, as Schürmann argues, at the end of the medieval tradition. In regard to the discussion in this paper, Leibniz provides what is probably the last 'image of creation,' and, as we can see, the first harbinger of the world we live in today in the form of the binary number system that drives modern computer science (see Figure 7.1).[4]

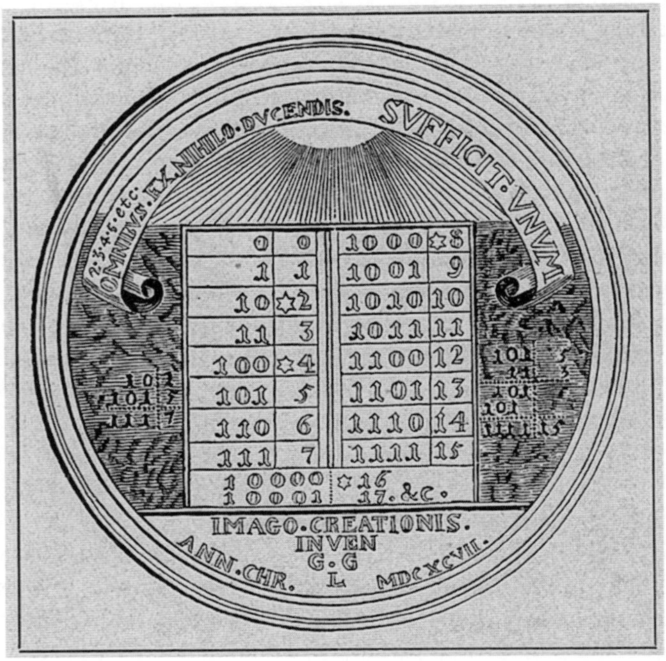

Figure 7.1 'The Image of Creation,' medallion designed by G. W. F. Leibniz depicting the binary number system.

The return of the image

By the end of the nineteenth century, the vision of the sciences had come to be characterized by a radical form of mechanism. To some degree this move in the sciences began with Leibniz's contemporaries, René Descartes and Isaac Newton, but by 1890, as Anne Harrington has outlined in her study of the German biological and cognitive sciences in the first part of the twentieth century (1996), the model of the machine had become the paradigm for normal science. Jung was clearly distressed by these developments. His distress can be seen in his participation in the Zofingia fraternity, where the presentations he made to his fellow students highlighted his objection to the dominant mechanistic model (Jung 1983). Among his targets of ridicule at that time was Emil Du Bois-Reymond, the leading proponent of strict mechanistic science. Jung's Zofingia lectures do not figure in Harrington's account of the development of a counter position characterized by arguments for a more holistic science in the German scientific world, but it is clear in reading them that Jung's sympathies lay with this movement. I will not at this point try to summarize all of Harrington's argument, but along with the additional cultural influences on Jung's writing of *The Red Book* that have already been highlighted in other chapters, I believe that her book, and the thinkers discussed in it, form an essential element in understanding the cultural environment within which Jung was working. Among the foremost advocates of the holistic position was Jakob von Uexküll, the founder of the modern science of ethology.

Von Uexküll's contribution to the anti-mechanistic, holistic view of the sciences of life and mind was the development of the notion of the *umwelt*. Although previous to his work the umwelt was taken to be a general reference to the environment, essentially an undifferentiated description of a given environmental state of affairs, von Uexküll reformulated the concept into a means of describing the unique environmental experience of a particular organism. Thus, in his books we can find depictions of the varying perceptual patterns of an adult and a child – simple perspectival variations – or the manner in which a fly would experience the same situation – characterized by the particular elements of the fly's perceptual apparatus. According to von Uexküll, any living organism enjoys its own distinctive umwelt, and the task of the scientist is to describe, in the greatest possible detail, the features of the organism's distinct unwelt. Only in this manner could the organism be properly understood. Von Uexküll's position shared a number of features with the work of the British comparative psychologist, Conway Lloyd Morgan, who is cited by Jung, and who, along with the American psychologist James Mark Baldwin, was a likely influence on Jung's engagement with evolutionary theory (Hogenson 2001).

This ethological point of view, which informed significant elements of the holistic movement described by Harrington, provides a context for understanding one of the more peculiar passages in Jung's *Collected Works*. In Jung's essay, 'On the Nature of the Psyche,' which I consider to be his most scientifically systematic discussion of his system of psychology, we find the following comment:

> In view of the structure of the body, it would be astonishing if the psyche were the only biological phenomenon not to show clear traces of its evolutionary history, and it is altogether probable that these marks are closely connected with the instinctual base. Instinct and archaic mode meets in the biological conception of the 'pattern of behavior.' There are, in fact, no amorphous instincts, as every instinct bears in itself the pattern of its situation. Always it fulfills an image, and the image has fixed qualities. The instinct of the leaf-cutting ant fulfills the image of ant, tree, leaf, cutting, transport, and little ant-garden of fungi. If any one of these conditions is lacking, the instinct does not function, because it cannot exist without its total pattern, without its image.
>
> (1954: par. 398)

Clearly, what Jung provides here is a description of the umwelt of the leaf-cutting ant. But Jung does not invoke von Uexküll's language, rather moving back to his own original interest in the image, now embedded in this biological example, in order to incorporate his vision of the psyche into a larger scientific, but also holistic, vision. Jung seeks to hold onto his reputation as a rigorous scientist, first established in his work on the word association test, while encompassing the insights he had gained in his work on active imagination and in the writing of *The Red Book*, which now begins to take on the qualities of an umwelt as well. I want to illustrate this last point by looking again at the very first illustration in *Liber Primus*.

The image, with which *The Red Book* begins, is a detailed depiction of a world (Plate 11). One could assume that a portion of the image is a depiction of a Swiss or German town with a prominent church or cathedral, lacking a cross, on the shore of a lake. Perhaps Lake Constance near Jung's birthplace. The only problem with this interpretation is what we find beneath the surface of the water, where jellyfish – the medusas and other aquatic creatures studied by Ernst Haeckel, which Joseph Cambray argues in Chapter 4 of this volume were a direct influence on the structure of Jung's images – and coral abound. These organisms are unlikely to be found in any body of fresh water, particularly in central Europe, but they are, as Cambray demonstrates, the likely inspiration for much of the design of the paintings in *The Red Book*. Arrayed above the town is the starry sky with the moon, planets, and the signs of the zodiac and the sun properly placed in the transitional space of the Platonic Month. To the left, in the upright portion of the first letter of the book is a crowned serpent emerging from a fiery vessel. Although the serpent is a recurrent figure in *The Red Book*, neither the marine figures nor the zodiacal signs are part of the narrative, although there are important allusions to the Platonic Month and Year, which rely on zodiacal progressions. Jung was, of course, deeply interested in these aspects of the calculation of time and had, at one point, upset Freud with his investigations of the horoscopes of his patients. There are also comments in Jung's autobiographical reflections concerning some interest in marine entities, and both Freud and Ernst Haeckel worked with marine animals in various stages of their scientific careers (Jung 1983). What we have then, in this initial image in *The Red Book* is a fairly extensive depiction of a variety of interests and influences that gave shape to Jung's life and thought. *The Red Book* is Jung's umwelt, and, as such, it represents Jung's recovery of the holistic image in the age of the sciences.

Coda

In 1952, the physicist Wolfgang Pauli published an essay, in conjunction with Jung's famous paper on synchronicity that examined the seventeenth-century debate between Robert Fludd and Johannes Kepler (Jung and Pauli 1955). In 1984, the historian of science Robert Westman contributed a paper to a conference on occult and scientific mentalities in the Renaissance held at the ETH in Zürich and entitled 'Nature, Art, and Psyche: Jung, Pauli, and the Kepler-Fludd Polemic' (Westman 1984). Westman remarks, at the beginning of his paper, that his investigations reveal,

> quite surprisingly . . . that there is a profound unity in the questions with which Kepler and Fludd were concerned and that the center of a cluster of apparently diverse issues lay in the problem of establishing the connections between pictures, words, and things.
>
> (1984: 178)

Fludd, Westman demonstrates, was deeply engaged in the study of images, drawing inspiration from the works of Albrecht Dürer, in particular, and preparing 'a systematic account of the visible and invisible world from the time of the Creation (and even before!)' (186). Kepler was also interested in the pictorial representation of nature and the soul, but, as Westman argues:

> One of the most famous pictures in the history of science, after all, is Kepler's nest of polyhedra, which purports to bear metaphysical, physical and mathematical meanings. To be precise, the polyhedra are images of God's archetypal Ideas, which he used to form the world in the best of all possible ways. Prior to these figures, both temporally and ontologically, came the image of God himself as a sphere. . . . But Kepler's and Fludd's Gods have different 'archetypal scripts' for the world. Kepler's guiding image is a point that flows ceaselessly in all planes to form a sphere; Fludd's picture is a point that is the vertex of a pyramid of Light, and is either mirrored symmetrically or opposed by an interpenetrating pyramid of Darkness. . . . Fludd is always seeking moral, spiritual, and pietistic connotations in the geometry and arithmetic used to construct his pictures. Kepler's nose is always pointed in the opposite direction. The archetypal baggage he carries away from his deity unpacks into physical images and geometrical structures, whose purpose is to explain and to justify the Copernican world to which he was already committed.
>
> (201–3)

Earlier in his paper, Westman, quoting Fludd, lays out the nature of his dispute with Kepler: 'The true philosophy,' Fludd writes, 'will diligently investigate heaven and earth, and will sufficiently explore, examine and depict Man, who is unique, by means of pictures [*imaginibus depinget*].' Westman comments:

> Now, though fragmentary, the phrase *imaginibus depinget* ('it will depict or portray by means of pictures') provides an important clue to the Kepler–Fludd polemic. Behind the strategies of personal polarization and the emotional language of contrasts and opposites

> that pervade the dispute with Kepler lay a real dispute about the meaning and reality of visual imaginings.
>
> (1984: 179)

As both Westman and Suzanne Gieser, in her detailed examination of the Pauli–Jung relationship (Gieser 2005) argue, this Renaissance argument was not incidental to Pauli's concerns in the development of quantum mechanics. Neils Bohr, who was a major figure in Pauli's life, maintained, along with Irwin Schrödinger, that theoretical formulations had to be amenable to some form of visualization – hence Bohr's notion of the atom as a small solar system. In contrast to this point of view, Werner Heisenberg argued in favor of a purely nonvisual, mathematical view of theoretical physics. As quantum mechanics advanced, this 'crisis of visualization' (Gieser 2005) became increasingly acute and certainly provides one frame of reference for Pauli's fascination with Jung's theory of archetypes, which, in at least some renderings, present an image of the world beyond consciousness, if not, finally, an image of creation.

Notes

1 In addition to developing Jung's visionary account, it is worth considering whether this exchange in *The Red Book* is also a foreshadowing of the argument in Jung's *Answer to Job*.

2 Sonu Shamdasani, editor of *The Red Book*, references Jung's Nietzsche Seminars (Jung 1988), where Jung discusses the ambiguity of the notion of the *übermensch* (see *The Red Book*, 2009: 243, n. 127). Clearly as scholarly assessment of *The Red Book* progresses, the meaning of *übersinn* will increasingly become a point of controversy (cf. Giegerich 2010).

3 This passage should evoke further reflection on the relationship between Jung's point of view and that of Lacan. As Jung struggles with the place of the image and the symbol in economy of the psyche, and the relationship of the symbolic to the scientific, Lacan's notion of the Real may shed light.

4 Leibniz struck this medallion to memorialize his discovery of the binary number system. For Leibniz, however, the number system retained elements of pre-Enlightenment mystical and theological significance. The inscription at the top of the medallion reads '*Omnibus ex nihilo ducendis sufficit unum*' (To make all things from nothing, unity suffices). Leibniz thus believed that the binary number system constituted a proof for the existence of the Christian God – unity could create everything from nothing – but also believed that the system revealed the unity of human understanding of the universe by way of the correspondence that appeared to exist between the binary system and the hexagrams in the Chinese *I Ching* or *Book of Changes* (Cajori 1916).

References

Cajori, Florian (1916) 'Leibniz's "Image of Creation,"' *The Monist*, 26: 557–65.

Diebold, William J. (2000) *Word and Image: An Introduction to Early Medieval Art*, Boulder: Westview Press.

Giegerich, Wolfgang (2010) 'Liber Novus, that is, the New Bible: A First Analysis of C. G. Jung's Red Book,' *Spring*, 83: 361–411.

Gieser, Suzanne (2005) *The Innermost Kernel: Depth Psychology and Quantum Physics, Wolfgang Pauli's Dialogue with C. G. Jung*, Berlin: Springer.

Harrington, Anne (1996) *Reenchanted Science: Holism in German Culture from Wilhelm II to Hitler*, Princeton: Princeton University Press.

Hogenson, George B. (1983) *Jung's Struggle with Freud*, Notre Dame: University of Notre Dame Press.

—— (2001) 'The Baldwin Effect: A Neglected Influence on C. G. Jung's Evolutionary Thinking,' *Journal of Analytical Psychology*, 46: 591–611.

Jung, C. G. (1954). 'On the Nature of the Psyche,' *The Archetypes and the Collective Unconscious, The Collected Works of C. G. Jung*, trans. R. F. C. Hull, vol. 8, 159–234. Princeton: Princeton University Press.

—— (1983) *The Zofingia Lectures*, trans. J. V. Heurck, Princeton: Princeton University Press.

—— (1988) *Nietzsche's Zarathustra: Notes of the Semimar Given in 1934–1939 by C. G. Jung*, Princeton: Princeton University Press.

—— (2009) *The Red Book: Liber Novus*, ed. S. Shamdasani, trans. M. Kyburz, J. Peck, and S. Shamdasani, New York: W. W. Norton & Company.

Jung, C. G., and Pauli, Wolfgang (1955) *The Interpretation of Nature and the Psyche. Synchronicity: An Acausal Connecting Principle*, New York: Pantheon Books.

Kitcher, Patricia (1995) *Freud's Dream: A Complete Interdisciplinary Science of Mind*, Cambridge, MA: The MIT Press.

Lacan, Jacques (2006) *Ecrits: The First Complete English Translation*, trans. B. Fink, New York: W. W. Norton.

Laplanche, J. and Pontalis, J.-B. (1973) *The Language of Psychoanalysis*, New York: W. W. Norton.

Marion, Jean-Luc (2004) *The Crossing of the Visible*, trans. J. K. A. Smith, Stanford: Stanford University Press.

Masson, Jefrey Moussaieff (ed.) (1985) *The Complete Letters of Sigmund Freud to Wilhelm Fliess 1887–1904*, Cambridge, MA: Harvard University Press.

Moran, Dermot (1989) *The Philosophy of John Scotus Eriugena: A Study of Idealism in the Middle Ages*, Cambridge: Cambridge University Press.

Ricoeur, Paul (1995) 'Manifestation and Proclamation,' trans. D. Pellauer, in M. I. Wallace (ed.), *Figuring the Sacred: Religion, Narrative, and Imagination*, 48–67, Minneapolis: Fortress Press.

Schürmann, Reiner (1978) *Meister Eckhart*, Bloomington: Indiana University Press.

—— (1987). *Heidegger on Being and Acting: From Principles to Anarchy*, trans. C.-M. Gros, Bloomington: Indiana University Press.

Stein, Murray (2008) '"Divinity expresses the self . . ." an investigation,' *Jounal of Analytical Psychology*, 53: 305–27.

Vattimo, Gianni (2006) *Dialogue with Nietzsche*, trans. W. McCuaig, New York: Columbia University Press.

Westman, Robert S. (1984) 'Nature, Art, and Psyche: Jung, Pauli, and the Kepler-Fludd Polemic,' in B. Vickers (ed.), *Occult and Scientific Mentalities in the Renaissance*, Cambridge: Cambridge University Press.

8

THE RED BOOK AS A WORK OF LITERATURE

John Beebe

Clinical Relevance

When psychology is taught in a conference setting, as was the case when this paper was first presented, authors are required to show that whatever they are propounding is relevant to the contemporary clinical treatment of patients. This is for a very practical reason: psychology conferences are normally offered for continuing education credit, and credit is given only if those attending will be made more effective doctors as a result of each presentation.

The subject of this paper is *The Red Book* as a work of literature, and I do strongly maintain that my presentation is neither frivolous nor merely academic. As required, in fact, it applies squarely to the treatment of patients. I examine the experience of reading *The Red Book* for its literary qualities in order to gain insight into what kind of book it is and its relation to Jung's later development of analytical psychology, which, of course, he applied to the healing of patients. I consider the psychologically picaresque quality of the narrative, its frequent evocations of other books, and its combination of mythological, theological, and philosophical development through a variety of narrative styles and voices as well as accompanying pictures. I discuss the tension between irony and prophecy that pervades the narrative and how these come together in a meditation on the nature of psychic distress and its healing through nonrational means, which deepens one genre to which this book is seminal – the psychological memoir.

The Red Book is a living memorial to the psychological experience of surviving the disorientation occasioned by the emergence of what Jung was later to term a 'psychic epidemic,' the affects associated with the arrival of World War I, which the book anticipates, verifies, and tries to work through. The turn to this kind of writing is not infrequently seen in patients who are struggling with complexes of past traumas, reawakened in the face of similar cultural conditions. Here, I show that, in common with the best of such work, Jung's *Red Book* dramatizes with skill not only the abreaction of the fragmented psychic state of one individual traumatized by historical upheaval, but also the therapeutic strategies for self-healing that can emerge out of such an experience. *The Red Book* thus provides in literary form a model of how the integrity of psyche can be restored in the face of cultural processes that threaten to undermine it.

The reader of this paper will become oriented to a literary work that was produced through the use of visionary defenses – the way that some individuals cope with emergent reactive stress syndrome with an outpouring of creativity in an attempt to rehearse symbolic solutions to the distresses surrounding them.[1] Readers may learn from the study of Jung's material ways to distinguish clinically between a spiritual crisis and a psychotic stress reaction. Readers will also discover the value of an individual developing the religious attitude of psyche in original, nondogmatic, creative ways in the midst of troubled times filled with collective turmoil.

Times of cultural disorientation form part of the cultural history of all groups. Recent examples in the United States include the attack on the World Trade Center, the devastation of New Orleans by Hurricane Katrina, and the Deepwater Horizon oil spill in the Gulf of Mexico. Such events are a source of concern and anxiety to many individuals, some of whom are led by them to work out a whole new spiritual orientation. As Gregory Bateson has shown, the human mind is exquisitely sensitive to phenomena that suggest the normal pattern of a culture is being, *or may soon be*, disrupted. The mind's first recourse may be a turn to vision that can help it become symbolically oriented to the changed realities it faces. The way Jung meets the trauma of his time and heals himself not only makes gripping reading but also provides a model that others can draw upon. Clinicians can learn from studying *The Red Book* to be more respectful of literary efforts that may spontaneously emerge in the midst of psychotherapy rather than reject them as resistances to the therapeutic work posed by gifted but controlling patients.

The Red Book as a trickster work of art

The Red Book takes us not only into the world of the Middle Ages, but also into the field of a midlife crisis. In my own early midlife, I started writing and publishing in the Jungian world with a paper called 'The Trickster in the Arts.' In that paper, I defined a trickster work of art as one that puts the person who experiences it in a double bind. A double bind is a problematic situation to which there seem to be only two potential solutions, neither of which turns out to be acceptable. An additional necessary condition of the double bind is that walking away from the situation is not an option.

The person who creates a trickster work of art is usually in a state of rage at the time of its composition. Literary work is often the safest and most productive means to discharge the rage. Some readers may have sensed in the first section of this very paper a tricksterish tinge, a protest on the narrowness with which our American medical establishment defines what is relevant for the continuing education of doctors.

Oddly enough, some of the world's best books have been written in a rageful, tricksterish state of mind. I might mention, for example, *Hamlet*, Henry James's gruesome novella, 'The Turn of the Screw,' and Herman Melville's *The Confidence Man*. I agree with Sonu Shamdasani's criticism that there has been a ridiculously Freudocentric interpretation of Jung's work, yet how can we leave out the state of mind that Jung must have been in at a personal level after his break with Freud? He refers to it as late as his eighty-second year, when, recalling the depreciation he experienced at the hands of Freud and the psychoanalytic school, he writes of 'the teeth of my resentment.'[2] At the beginning of the *Scrutinies* section of *Liber Novus* in the present edition of *The Red Book*, Jung gives voice to the feelings he had on the day that he resigned as president of the International Psychoanalytic Association. Dialoguing with himself, Jung says,

> You want to complain about others, and that one has done an injustice to you, not understood you, misinterpreted you, hurt your feelings, ignored you, not recognized you, falsely accused you, and what else? Do you see your vanity in this, your eternally ridiculous vanity?
>
> (333)[3]

The experience of reading *The Red Book* definitely includes, even if in the background, an apprehension of the affect of rage, an anger that may have taken the form of an agitated depression. I never feel in reading *The Red Book* that Jung verged toward any kind of psychosis, but I do sense that he was suffering from an affective disorder. Jung could become hypomanic and was, at times, quite irritable. He sometimes had trouble recognizing his emotions as emotions, something I don't find uncommon in people whose dominant mode of consciousness is introverted intuition and whose auxiliary function is extraverted thinking, which is how I see Jung. In such an orientation, not only is the introverted feeling function a bit in the background, but even more removed is the introverted sensation that could help to locate in the body exactly what is being experienced at a particular moment in time. Feelings and bodily sensations catch the intuitive-thinking type from behind. It makes sense to me that in such a person rage could be channeled and very gradually processed through the creation of a tricksterish work of art. For this reason, *The Red Book* is not quite in the genre of psychological memoir. Unlike *Memories, Dreams, Reflections*, it is written in the heat of encounter with the unconscious, rather than recounted and interpreted from a safe distance.

The trickster work of art is one that never quite conforms to an established genre. It breaks the boundary of literary form. The reader has the peculiar feeling that to meet and digest the work will be of the greatest value, and yet that it may be all but impossible to do so. The translators of *The Red Book* in its present English edition mention 'the considerable anomaly of the language that Jung had to find through sleepless nights from 1913 onward. That language shifted its shape, altered its scale, and weighed both megrims and tons' (223). They identify 'three main stylistic registers': 'One of them faithfully reports the fantasies and inner dialogues of Jung's imaginal encounters, while a second remains firmly and discerningly conceptual. Still a third writes in a mantic and prophetic, or Romantic and dithyrambic, mode' (222).

None of these 'registers' was easy to translate, and none entirely easy to read. Further, as Sonu Shamdasani was the first to uncover, there are normally two layers to the text:

> Jung each time sets down an initial protocol layer of narrative encounter, usually with dialogue, and then in the 'second layer,' a lyrical elaboration of and commentary on that encounter. The first layer avoids an elevated tone, whereas the second welcomes elevation and modulations into sermonic, mantic-prophetic reflections on the episode's meaning, which in turn unpack events discursively.
>
> (222)

Jung introduced still another layer to *The Red Book* in the form of paintings that in more than one style depict allegories not fully explained in the text. These paintings can be deceptive and difficult to decipher. Moreover, even when carefully contemplating just one of these registers and layers by focusing on a few sentences or a single image, there is no shortcut to the psychic payoff that is apprehended. A single paragraph can leave one alternately exhilarated and obtunded in the face of its profound ambiguities. One senses instantly that reading a précis of the trickster work of art will not be at all a useful substitute for the experience of suffering its indignities one page at a time.

The sheer size and weight of *The Red Book* make it difficult to read. Sonu Shamdasani advised me to get a lectern and read it standing up. Thinking myself clever, I bought two lecterns so I could read the English while having the corresponding German page open beside me. Almost immediately, I was thwarted. Unlike Goethe, who could read and write standing up, I found that I couldn't. Next, I brought the book to bed and was soon flattened beneath it. Nevertheless, I had already seen enough that my curiosity was hooked. Finally, like a psychoanalytic patient, I absorbed it on the couch. I suffered every possible inconvenience until, somehow, it became a book I could read. In the physical misery it caused, the trickserish double bind is easy to see: you can't manage the book this way, but you can't read it that way, and you certainly can't just put it away.

Senex spirit in *The Red Book*

The Red Book isn't only a trickster work of art. It also gives considerable voice to the *senex*. The term *senex* sneaked into the archetypal list rather late in the game. A German literary scholar, Ernst Robert Curtius (1886–1956), had noted a certain trope in late Latin literature in which a boy (*puer*) and old man (*senex*) would appear together, sometimes in the same person (*puer senilis*, or *senex puer*) (Curtius 1990: 98–101). One recalls Leonardo's famous *Old Man and Young Man* (1495–1500). Senex means 'old man' and is the Latin root of 'senator'. In 1967, in the midst of the youth revolution of that time, James Hillman wrote the seminal essay on this archetype ('Senex and Puer: An Aspect of the Historical and Psychological Present.'[4] Among other things, Hillman saw in the senex the image of Saturn and what the Wilhelm/Baynes translation of the *I Ching* names *Limitation*. Saturn, with his sickle, is the God of Death who cuts things down. At the very least, he casts a cold, disapproving eye. Jung had complained of the senex in Sigmund Freud, especially in his last letter to Freud (18 December 1912) where, in a remarkable display of tricksterish extraverted feeling, Jung basically provoked Freud into breaking off their relationship.

One of the insights in Hillman's essay is that the senex archetype has been very important for Jungian psychology. It has somehow been transmuted into the wise, rather than merely dismissive, old man, at times embodied in Jung himself and echoed in the pronouncements against the irresponsibility of the puer that we associate with Marie Louise von Franz (1970a; 1970b). In *The Red Book*, we find both kinds of senex – the wise and the sere. More than a few pages are spent in tedious, scholastic philosophizing. Sometimes I felt I would die if I had to read more of them. Actually, I would be interested to see an edition of *The Red Book* that leaves out Jung's commentary on what the inner encounters mean and just gives us the 'screenplay.' At the same time, the book contains many pieces of authentic, interesting wisdom. What a deconstruction at the feeling level is required to experience the book!

Readers will notice the remarkable tension that is held in the work between the *bonhomie* of the trickster – the cleverness of Jung and the wit of some of the inner figures, particularly the Red One and Salome, at times an anima figure who clearly has already integrated the trickster – and the severity of the senex, felt, for example, in Ammonius the Anchorite, who makes his home in the desert. The Librarian is a similarly self-limiting character. The interesting thing about the book is how it *holds* this tension between trickster and senex. This is one way in which I slightly disagree with Hillman: I feel that the opposition of senex and puer is not nearly as interesting as the tension between senex and trickster.

Disguised novel

For a number of years, I participated in a reading group in which we read only 'odd' books. We didn't plan it that way; it's just how it worked out. One of the odd books was Stendhal's *On Love*. *On Love* is a long philosophical treatise about love, yet if you spend enough time with it, you begin to see that it is a novel in disguise. *The Red Book*, in its way, can be seen as a novel in disguise. Jung too, after all, confronted the possibility that it could be published as a literary work somewhere between memoir and fiction.[5]

As I've thought about the oddness of *The Red Book* and about the tension between senex and trickster, I've had an uneasy sense that I've experienced this combination before. It dawned on me that I had met that senex/trickster pairing in *Don Quixote*, in which the trickster Sancho Panza accompanies the aged Don Quixote on his strange quest. Don Quixote has unbalanced his mind by dwelling too long in the fantasy world of medieval romances. One way to look at *Don Quixote* is as a metaphor for the work that Spain had to do to absorb and integrate its decline after the defeat of the Spanish Armada in 1588. Spain had to realize that it would not be possible to sustain its heroic phase. *Don Quixote* makes fun of the very attempt to do so. Today one sees in American politics the senex and trickster coming together to try to keep the illusion of America as heroic nation alive (Beebe 2007: 275–96).

Is *The Red Book* post-heroic?

Propping up an exhausted hero is not at all what Jung is doing in this novel, if I may call it that. He tells us in the first book of *Liber Novus* that, with the help of a youthful figure, he has murdered Siegfried, the German hero (241–2). This signals a post-heroic story. In his 1925 seminar on analytical psychology, given in English, Jung explains what this hero seems to have meant to him (seems, because even he was surprised that this traditional figure mattered enough that Jung had to kill him off before he could begin the journey of connecting with his soul):

> The hero, as I told you, is the symbol of the greatest value recognized by us. Christ has been our hero when we accept the principles of his life as our own principles. Or Herakles or Mithras becomes my hero when I am determined to be as disciplined as they were. So it appeared as if Siegfried were my hero. I felt an enormous pity for him, as though I myself had been shot. I must then have had a hero I did not appreciate, and it was my ideal of force and efficiency I had killed. I had killed my intellect . . . deposed my superior function.
>
> (Jung 1989: 57)

The hero role, when Jung had been active first as Eugen Bleuler's chief assistant and then as Freud's chief general, leading well-planned campaigns to conquer the psychological and psychiatric establishment for psychoanalysis, had necessarily required him to become interested in efficiency. In his Freudian period, alongside his private practice, Jung had to manage being a writer, editor, and lecturer communicating nearly nonstop with well-placed international colleagues on both sides of the Atlantic. It was therefore necessary for him to draw upon an archetype that was capable of promoting efficiency. As *Liber Novus* begins, however, Jung's insight is that instead of drawing once more on his capacity for mastery, to reconnect with the soul he had left behind in this pursuit of medical power, he is going to have to make an effort to catch hold of his *incapacity*.

The dream of murdering Siegfried came to Jung on the first anniversary of the day that he wrote the letter to Freud that provoked the end of their relations. As other psychological writers have noted (Beebe 2010: 42–4), the mythical Siegfried is the son of King Sigmund. I have read a popular account of the heroic Siegfried, written in 1912, that describes him on horseback, bearing a shield with a crown on it (Mackenzie 1912/2010). He was the Crown Prince. In his time, Jung was himself called the Crown Prince of the psychoanalytic movement. What he is killing in the dream is his role as heir apparent of the psychoanalytic movement – his sonship to Freud. For all the reasons outlined in George Hogenson's paper,[6] Freud's psychoanalysis had become too limiting for Jung.

This dream of assassination speaks to Jung's ambivalent feelings over the abrupt, perhaps unanticipated, sacrifice he has made of just this level of efficient striving in the service of his career. Then, in the outer world, a Crown Prince, heir to the Austro-Hungarian Empire, is killed and world war begins. Jung was able to see that personal complex and cultural complex had converged, and that his own ambition had fallen in line with a one-sidedness in the emphasis of his time to which history itself was now offering a violent compensation. Hard as it was for Jung to give up the role of Crown Prince, he could feel, taking the lesson from the collective example, that it was right for him to do so. The times were demanding, as if from within themselves, that the heroic quest for a brilliant adaptation be sacrificed. I have argued that *The Red Book* was, in this sense, a work of conscience (Beebe 2010: 40–58), to hold the sacrifice in consciousness, rather than letting the hero be sacrificed again and again through unconsciousness, as was happening at that time on a thousand European battlefields. Through the interplay of senex and trickster that he depicts in *The Red Book*, Jung opened an alternative way, a consciousness in himself that moved beyond the hero, or at least beyond the hero that serves only what he calls 'the spirit of this time' (229 ff.).

What emerges is a different kind of heroic journey from the ones we are used to. This time, its direction is not up toward mastery, but down into a profound acceptance of incapacity, a descent into the unconscious requiring essential support from the anima. Nor is this, as in *Wandlungen und Symbole der Libido*, a quest for knowledge, an exploration of the collective unconscious that charts the path of a hero rescuing psychological consciousness from the pre-Oedipal mother. Rather, there is a sacrifice of the pretense to knowing throughout, starting with a refusal to insist on the kind of knowing that can be supported solely by science. A key moment is Jung's encounter with Gilgamesh (here called Izdubar). Notice the striking verticality of the image of Izdubar in *The Red Book* (36)! There is a strong sense of spine, of a man standing very upright. Elsewhere, I have written about uprightness as a symbol of integrity and have advanced the idea of the connection between the superior and inferior functions as the 'spine' of personality (Beebe 1992). We speak of someone as being straight as an arrow or having a ramrod sense of morality. When Jung receives gifts from Salome,[7] one is a straight metal rod, which symbolically reinforces the strength of the connection that is developing between ego and anima (307).

Between 1913 and 1920, Jung's theory of psychological types developed strikingly. In 1913, when he was still president of the International Psychoanalytic Association, Jung thought that there were only two types: introverted thinking and extraverted feeling. Both were rational, used for evaluating and decision making. By the time he wrote *Psychological Types*, the theory had expanded to include four functions of consciousness: the two rational ones and two that were functions of perception, the irrational functions of sensation and intuition. We can see this opening out of the theory developing in *The Red Book*, especially the work on the irrational axis of consciousness. Jung refers to this axis as magic or at least as enabling him to get to magic.[8]

It seems to me that when he takes the upright, intuitive Izdubar, who (as Gilgamesh) was a culture hero operating within the magical worldview of the cosmos held by the ancient Sumerians, and practically lays him flat with the news that the world isn't flat, Jung is confronted with the damage that rationality can cause to the irrational axis of consciousness: it can rob it of its claim to integrity. That is why Jung goes to such lengths, I believe, to rebirth the hero in an egg of his own creation until he can be reconstituted as a god, a dominant of consciousness (Izdubar emerges as the sun), a process that establishes once and for all an irrational function as Jung's chief orientation to his life's work, the exploration of the unconscious. When he agrees to receive the magical rod from Salome, he is accepting the irrational spine of his own authentic psychology, his true psychological type, and that enables him finally to accept once more a crown – not the crown of Siegfried, but of the god of the frogs, Abraxas, who symbolizes the irrational power of Nature itself. Here, we have a fantastic vision of a transcending superior function and a descending inferior function, both irrational in the sense of being simply given, not judged, in one embodied creature, emphasizing the need to have both (as did the Christ who Jung wants to imitate, who knew he must, to incarnate fully as the redeemer, go both up to Heaven and down to Hell).

The key to Jung's establishing his moral spine of personality is the consistent emphasis in *The Red Book* on the embrace of incapacity, the search for the soul that embodies the inferior function. This is a new, deeply psychologically informed, kind of hero's journey, in the sense of forging a new path that will fully enable Jung to abandon all earlier heroes' fantasies of mastery: to discover how to hold one's capacity in tension with one's incapacity. The journey is kept on its downward track to authentic personality grounding through the intervention of the trickster and the senex.

Here is Jung talking to the knavish Red One (259):

> 'Who are you?'
>
> 'Who am I? You think I am the devil. Do not pass judgment. Perhaps you can also talk to me without knowing who I am. What sort of a superstitious fellow are you, that immediately you think of the devil?'

Before long, Jung says,

> 'You make me curious. You seem to be a rare breed. Your appearance is not ordinary, and then too – forgive me – it seems to me that you bring with you a strange air, something worldly, something impudent, or exuberant, or – in fact – something pagan.'

A bit later, the Red One remarks,

> 'You're an unbelievably ponderous and serious person. Are you always so urgent?'

I see in this dialogue the seeds of Jung's decision not to adopt the Zarathustra style for *Liber Novus*. He is eschewing the kind of transcendentalism that, through Emerson, informed Nietzsche. Instead of the inflation of the curious seeker of truth, the Red One bids Jung to develop his sense of humor, inviting him to come down to earth. In terms of the psychological types that I see involved in this dialogue, Jung's priggish, rather pietistic, puer introverted feeling is getting its comeuppance from a very skillful, tricksterish extraverted feeling that knows how to handle him!

This interchange is followed, before very long, by a meeting with Ammonius the Anchorite, who exemplifies the senex archetype (267–72). Still later (275–6), we learn that the Red One and Ammonius, who had seemed to be totally unknown to each other, are, in fact, traveling together – like Sancho Panza and Don Quixote. They're embarrassed to be seen together by Jung!

Philemon and Salome: Limitation and realism

It is through the figure of Philemon, the wise, old Stoic magician who is content to tend his own garden, that the senex comes into its own in the narrative. With reluctance, Philemon is drawn into Jung's service. He helps the modern searcher and thinker formulate what he has been learning about the irrational. Because Philemon looks like a prophet, it is tempting to say that he might embody Jung's introverted intuition. Instead, I'd say that what we see in Philemon is powerful introverted thinking. Especially in the 'Seven Sermons to the Dead,' Philemon expounds a theory that successfully answers the enormous agitation of the Anabaptists.

The Anabaptists, who seem so concrete in their perceptions, carry the consciousness of Jung's demonic, least developed function of consciousness, introverted sensation. They are mightily disturbed that going to Jerusalem has not resulted in their finding what they wanted.

In actual history, the Anabaptists, who arose in the shadow of the Peasants' War of 1524–5, tried idealistically to create a New Jerusalem in which rather than mandatory infant baptism, baptism would be reserved until adulthood when Christian faith could be freely chosen. This movement began in Zurich, and its first martyr, Felix Mantz, who had initially been an enthusiastic student of Ulrich Zwingli, the founder of the Swiss Reformed Church (to which Jung belonged), was, for such free-thinking embrace of individual conscience, 'taken out on a boat on Lake Zurich where, bound with ropes, he was thrown overboard and drowned' (Liechty 1994: 17). The German Peasants' War is often seen as the broadest popular uprising occasioning the greatest loss in life in Europe prior to the French Revolution. The Anabaptists, whose desire for religious freedom within a Christian frame anticipates Jung's own, are emblematic of the collective complexes that can be activated in times of cultural stress, in this case the Reformation, which opened the question of how much individual conscience could challenge the authority of the traditional church in the effort to restore the integrity of Christian faith.

This cultural complex had been reactivated in Jung's life[9] from the moment that Nietzsche declared God was dead, which was nearly simultaneous with Jung's own father's loss of faith. On a more personal level, therefore, I think the Anabaptist horde represents Jung's agitated depression at the time of undertaking his effort to reconnect with his soul, which had a very concrete side, an undermining agitation around what could actually satisfy him that may have echoed what his father suffered through losing his Christian faith. I would call this a demonic introverted sensation, an insistence of concrete sensory verification that would not be satisfied with a religious view that was not based on inner facts. It fell to Jung to do what his introverted feeling father couldn't do, which was to heal himself by coming up with a new way of thinking about religion and the cosmos. That included his insistence, not on the kind of facts the dead Anabaptists seemed to want, but on the reality of the psyche.

Despite Jung's reservations about his ability to command such a reality in a literary form, *The Red Book* is, in part, like an autobiographical novel describing the experiences that built his new cosmology so that it becomes a sort of *bildungsroman*, a novel of formation or of education, not of the young man learning to develop a persona, but of the middle-aged man finally learning how to live with himself. Philemon uses his clear thinking to help Jung set limits on his anxieties. Many people who come to psychotherapy are seeking more than just to talk about their feelings. They actually need a philosophy of life. Jung understood this and led the way in the self-analysis recounted in *The Red Book*.

Salome's realism

One of the most remarkable aspects of *The Red Book* is the realism with which it treats the psyche. The anima, Salome, incarnates Jung's inferior extraverted sensation. One sees this in her seductive dance in the Biblical story and in the concreteness with which she demands the head of John the Baptist, a concreteness that is emphasized still more in Oscar Wilde's famous dramatic treatment, where the head of the holy man who had earlier refused her request that he kiss her is brought to the young woman on a platter and she takes it off, still dripping blood, in her own hands, bringing the dead mouth to hers, saying (in French) 'I have kissed your lips, John.'[10] In *The Red Book*, she takes things as they are and meets them in the moment. Eventually, we learn that she has been motivating most of the events in the book. Certainly, she must be behind Jung's ability to spontaneously do the active imagination, to be actually present to the inner figures.

If we can accept the extraverted sensation of this figure that is identified as Jung's soul, and see her as mediating the experience of the unconscious to him in a real and tangible way, as the muse informing his active imaginations throughout, we can see why Jung came to describe the archetypes not so much as dynamic issues, as he might have done in an archetypal extension of psychoanalytic theory, but as 'just-so' stories that must be experienced, enjoyed, and engaged with. The novelistic import of *The Red Book* is that our inner worlds are composed of such stories.[11] We have to accept them exactly as they are. The trickster reminds us to regard our own stories with a measure of irony and humor. The senex makes us skeptical and reminds us of the limits of what we can expect to integrate.

The last scene I'd like to recall from this often ironic, novelistic book is the exchange between Salome and Jung, in which Jung, trying to follow his Christian law of love into an unrestrainedly positive attitude toward what the soul may offer says to Salome (305), 'I will accept what you give. I do not have the right to judge or to reject.'

It is as if he is denying having a feeling function that might evaluate what he is given.

Salome replies,

> 'So listen. There is old armor and the rusty gear of our fathers down here, murderous leather trappings hanging from them, worm-eaten lance shafts, [we're right in *Don Quixote*!] twisted spear heads, broken arrows, rotten shields, skulls, the bones of man and horse, old cannons, catapults, crumbling firebrands, smashed assault gear, stone spearheads, stone clubs, sharp bones, chipped arrowhead teeth – everything the battles of yore have littered the earth with. Will you accept all this?'

Jung affirms, 'I accept it. You know better, my soul.' Here, Jung appears a very young soul! Now that he has killed off the hero, there's quite a boy left in his place. He has a lot to learn.

Salome says,

> 'I find painted stones, carved bones with magical signs, talismanic sayings on hanks of leather and small plates of lead, dirty pouches filled with teeth, human hair and fingernails, timbers lashed together, black orbs, moldy animal skins – all the superstitions hatched by dark prehistory. Will you accept all this?'

'I accept it all, how should I dismiss anything?' is Jung's reply.

Salome continues,

> 'But I find worse: fratricide, cowardly mortal blows, torture, child sacrifice, the annihilation of whole peoples, arson, betrayal, war, rebellion – will you also accept this?'

'Also this, if it must be. How can I judge?'

'I find epidemics, natural catastrophes, sunken ships, razed cities, frightful feral savagery, famines, human meanness, and fear, whole mountains of fear.'

'So shall it be since you give it.'

Then she says,

> 'I find the treasures of all past cultures, magnificent images of Gods, spacious temples, paintings, papyrus rolls, sheets of parchment with the characters of bygone languages, books full of lost wisdom, hymns and chants of ancient priests, stories told down the ages through thousands of generations.'

'This is an entire world – whose extent I cannot grasp,' cries Jung. 'How can I accept it?' (305–6).

At last Jung's common sense asserts itself!

Salome teases him. 'But you wanted to accept everything? You do not know your limits. Can you not limit yourself?'

'I must limit myself,' says Jung. 'Who could ever grasp such wealth?'

'Be content and cultivate your garden with modesty,' advises Salome.

This last benediction reminds us of *Candide*. Jung kept a bust of Voltaire in his waiting room. Making one's garden grow, knowing one's limits – in this gesture *The Red Book* surpasses its identity as a trickster work of art and, shifting genre again, speaks its integrity in a more straightforward way.

Notes

1 I have previously discussed visionary defenses in relation to cultural trauma in an (as yet) unpublished paper (Beebe 2005).

2 'Despite the blatant misjudgment I have suffered at Freud's hands, I cannot fail to recognize, even in the teeth of my resentment, his significance as a cultural critic and psychological pioneer.' From a letter written originally in German to Edith Schröder MD, *c.* April 1957 (Adler and Jaffe 1975: 359).

3 Page numbers in parentheses, without other identification, are from Jung (2009).

4 This essay, originally presented at an Eranos Conference, can now be found in Hillman's *Puer Papers* (1979: 3–53).

5 In a section of his Introduction to the present edition of *The Red Book: Liber Novus*, entitled 'Publication Deliberations,' Sonu Shamdasani tells us that 'from 1922 onward, in addition to discussions with Emma Jung and Toni Wolff, Jung had extensive discussions with Cary Baynes and Wolfgang Stockmayer concerning what to do with *Liber Novus*.' Shamdasani records an unsent letter, dated 2 October 1922, from Baynes to Jung reprising some things he had told her, apparently during one of her analytic hours, in which he had mentioned certain parallels to what he was doing, at least in terms of content, to that of the visionary novelist, Gustav Meyrink, author of *The Golem*:

> In another book of Meyrink's [,] the 'White Dominican,' you said he made use of exactly the same symbolism that had come to you in the first vision that revealed to your unconscious. Furthermore you said, he had spoken of a 'Red Book' which contained certain mysteries and the book that you are writing about the unconscious, you have called the 'Red Book.' Then you said you were in doubt as to what to do about that book. Meyrink you said could throw his into novel form and it was all right, but you could only command the scientific and philosophical method and that stuff you couldn't cast into that mold. I said you could use the Zarathustra form and you said that was true, but you were sick of that. I am too. Then you said you had thought of making an autobiography out of it. That would seem to me by far the best, because then you would tend to write as you spoke which was in a very colorful way. But apart from any difficulty with the form, you said you dreaded making it public because it was like selling your house.
>
> (212)

The Translators' Note to the present edition, by Mark Kyburz, John Peck, and Shamdasani, states:

> *Liber Novus* was coeval with the literary ferment that Mikhail Bakhtin called the dialogical prose imagination. The Anglo-Welsh writer and artist David Jones . . . referred to the rupture of the First World War, and its effects on the historical

sense of writers, artists, and thinkers, simply as 'The Break.' In concert with other experimental writing from these decades, *Liber Novus* excavates archaeological layers of literary adventure, with hard-won consciousness as both shovel and precious shard. While Jung actively considered publishing *Liber Novus* for many years, he chose not to make a name for himself in this literary manner (222–3).

6 In this volume, above, pp. 94–107.
7 See 'The Gift of Magic,' in *Liber Secundus* of *The Red Book* (307).
8 See Jung's comment near the end of 'The Gift of Magic':

> The nature of the way is magical, as are supplication and invocation . . .. Magic is the working of men on men, but your magic action does not affect your neighbor; it affects you first, and only if you withstand it does an invisible effect pass from you to your neighbor. There is more of it in the air than I ever thought. However, it cannot be grasped.
>
> (308)

I take this as a description of irrational consciousness.

9 Cultural complexes that have been repressed in former times can reappear, as Samuel Kimbles has suggested (2003: 222–3), as the 'transgenerational phantoms' described by Abraham and Torok (1994). I associate the reemergence of such 'phantoms' with the spooky 'haunting' of Jung's house in 1916 by the 'dead,' who when asked by Jung in an active imagination to speak, 'cried in many voices, "We have come back from Jerusalem, where we did not find what we sought. We implore you to let us in"' (346). Shamdasani's note 79 identifies these phantoms with the dead Anabaptists encountered by Jung in his active imagination of 17 January 1914, who 'led by Ezechiel were heading to Jerusalem to pray at the holy places' (294). This led to the delivery of the 'Seven Sermons of the Dead,' which the *Scrutinies* section of the present edition of *Liber Novus* assigns to Philemon. For the identification of the Dead's 'Jerusalem' with the New Jerusalem of the Anabaptists' political ambitions, enacted during the Peasants' War in several German cities such as Munster where, to Martin Luther's horror, economic class distinctions were for a time eliminated, which, of course, led to this branch of the Protestant movement's violent overthrow, see Shamdasani and Beebe (2010: 426–7).
10 As a student of type, I cannot see such behavior as an expression of extraverted feeling, which is how Jung typed this figure (1989: 88–90).
11 'What the unconscious expresses is far from being merely arbitrary or opinionated; it is something that happens to be "just-so," as is the case with every other natural being.' (Jung 1968: 17).

References

Abraham, N., and Torok, M. (1994) *The Shell and the Kernel*, Chicago, IL: University of Chicago Press.

Adler, G. and Jaffé, A. (eds) (1975) *C. G. Jung Letters*, vol. 2, R. F.C. Hull (trans.), Princeton: Princeton University Press.

Beebe, J. (1981) 'The Trickster in the Arts,' *San Francisco Jung Institute Library Journal*, 2(2): 22–54.

—— (1992) *Integrity in Depth*, College Station, TX: Texas A & M University Press.

—— (ed.) (2003) *Terror, Violence and the Impulse to Destroy: Perspectives from Analytical Psychology*, Papers from the 2002 North American Conference of Jungian Analysts and Candidates, Einsiedeln, Switzerland: Daimon Verlag.

—— 'Trauma and Psychological Creativity,' paper presented at the International Psychoanalytic Association Congress, Rio de Janeiro, July 28, 2005.
—— (2007) 'The Memory of the Hero and the Emergence of the Post-Heroic Attitude,' *Spring Journal*, 78, *Politics & the American Soul:* 275–96.
—— (2010) '*The Red Book* as a Work of Conscience,' *Quadrant*, 40(2): 40–58.
Cervantes, Miguel de (1605 and 1615/2003) *Don Quixote*, trans. Edith Grossman, New York: Ecco Press.
Curtius, E. R. (1990) *European Literature and the Latin Middle Ages*, 2nd edn, Princeton: Princeton University Press.
Hillman, J. (ed.) (1979) *Puer Papers*, Dallas, TX: Spring Publications.
Jung, C. G. (1912) *Wandlungen und Symbolen der Libido: Beiträge zur Entwicklungsgeschichte des Denkens*, Leipzig & Vienna: Franz Deuticke.
—— (1968) *Psychology and Alchemy, 2nd Edition, The Collected Works of C. G. Jung*, vol. 12, trans. R. F. C. Hull, Princeton: Princeton University Press.
—— (1989) *Analytical Psychology: Notes of the Seminar Given in 1925*, ed. W. McGuire, Princeton: Princeton University Press.
—— (2009) *The Red Book: Liber Novus*, trans. Sonu Shamdasani, Mark Kyburz, and John Peck, New York: W. W. Norton.
Kimbles, S. (2003) 'Cultural Complexes and Collective Shadow Processes,' in J. Beebe (ed.) *Terror, Violence and the Impulse to Destroy: Perspectives from Analytical Psychology*, Papers from the 2002 North American Conference of Jungian Analysts and Candidates, Einsiedeln, Switzerland: Daimon Verlag.
Liechty, D. (ed.) (1994) *Early Anabaptist Spirituality: Selected Writings*, New York: Paulist Press.
Mackenzie, D. (1912) *Teutonic Myth and Legend*, London: Gresham Publications.
Shamdasani, S. and Beebe, J. (2010) 'Jung becomes Jung: A Dialogue on *Liber Novus* (*The Red Book*),' *Psychological Perspectives*, 53(4): 410–36.
Von Franz, M. L. (1970a) *The Problem of the Puer Aeternus*, New York: Spring Publications.
—— (1970b) *A Psychological Interpretation of* The Golden Ass *of Apuleius*, New York: Spring Publications.
Wilde, O. (1891/1967) *Salome: A Play in One Act*, New York: Dover Publications.

INDEX

Chapters of *The Red Book* are indexed under the section in which they occur, either *Liber Primus* or *Liber Secundus*